Praise for *The Green Burial Guidebook*

"The landscape of death care is shifting, and Elizabeth Fournier is a wonderful guide. She brings us gently through green burials, home funerals, and more. *The Green Burial Guidebook* is essential for anyone planning for a sustainable death-care experience."

— **Katrina Spade,** founder of Recompose

"*The Green Burial Guidebook* is an engaging primer for first-timers looking to understand the fundamentals of the rapidly changing world of end-of-life and after-death care practices and possibilities. Through firsthand stories and insider savvy, Elizabeth Fournier has laid out some of the most doable, practical steps, choices, and skills you will need for planning your final affair. Thoughtful, well organized, and easy to take in."

— **Lee Webster,** home funeral and green burial advocate and editor of *Changing Landscapes: Exploring the Growth of Ethical, Compassionate, and Environmentally Sustainable Green Funeral Service*

"Elizabeth Fournier continues to help change the landscape of death care as we know it today. A wonderful guide for the layperson and funeral professional alike, *The Green Burial Guidebook* is a comprehensive treasure trove of information and personal experiences. It sheds light on the cemetery industry and the grassroots movement that seeks to return after-death care to what it used to be: families lovingly caring for their deceased in a final act of kindness. Bravo!"

— **Ed Bixby,** president of the Green Burial Council and owner of Steelmantown Cemetery and Purissima Natural Burial G̶r̶o̶

"Elizabeth Fournier introduces *T̶*
ple, straightforward guide,' and it
book is lovely, thoughtful, and b
the gracious guide at your side. Sh
to make a loved one's green burial b̶   ̶p̶l̶a̶n̶n̶i̶n̶g̶ and down-to-earth.

The *what, when, where, why, who,* and *how*? She's got them covered. Read *The Green Burial Guidebook* not only for all you'll learn but for the message of hope and joy it brings."

— **Mary Woodsen,** founding president of
Greensprings Natural Cemetery Preserve and
advisory board member of the Green Burial Council

"A straightforward handbook on more sustainable and meaningful death care in the United States and how to plan for it."

— **Suzanne Kelly, PhD,** author of *Greening Death:*
Reclaiming Burial Practices and Restoring Our Tie to the Earth

"Elizabeth Fournier's *Green Burial Guidebook* will change the way you think about death. The book is an informative and consoling read, offering tips and tools that will endure through the years. Fournier speaks with candor and kindness, as if she were seated right beside us at our kitchen table. She teaches about the realities and sacred possibilities in green burial, offering a life-affirming guide for those who wish to have a deeper connection to the earth, to the natural processes of life and death, and to their beloveds."

— **Lisa Smartt,** author of *Words at the Threshold* and
founder of the Final Words Project (www.finalwordsproject.org)

"*The Green Burial Guidebook* speaks to one of the deepest responsibilities of being human: caring for and burying our dead. This friendly guide will help you consider how your approach to death can be kinder to the earth and leave your community stronger."

— **Holly Pruett,** life-cycle celebrant, home funeral guide,
and Death Talk Project founder (www.hollypruettcelebrant.com
and www.deathtalkproject.com)

"Truly everything you need to plan a green send-off. A lively, informative, and uplifting book."

— **Mark Harris,** author of *Grave Matters: A Journey through*
the Modern Funeral Industry to a Natural Way of Burial

the

GREEN BURIAL GUIDEBOOK

the GREEN BURIAL GUIDEBOOK

Everything You Need to Plan
an Affordable, Environmentally Friendly Burial

ELIZABETH FOURNIER

New World Library
Novato, California

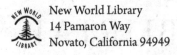
New World Library
14 Pamaron Way
Novato, California 94949

The material in this book is intended for education. It is not meant to take the place of legal advice from a licensed attorney.

Text design by Tona Pearce Myers

Library of Congress Cataloging-in-Publication data is available.

First printing, May 2018
ISBN 978-1-60868-523-3
Ebook ISBN 978-1-60868-524-0
Printed in Canada on 100% postconsumer-waste recycled paper

New World Library is proud to be a Gold Certified Environmentally Responsible Publisher. Publisher certification awarded by Green Press Initiative. www.greenpressinitiative.org

10   9   8   7   6   5   4   3

*In loving remembrance of my gentle parents
who shine their light on me from above.
I am truly nothing without you.*

CONTENTS

❧

INTRODUCTION

Death is an integral part of life, as natural and predictable as being born. But whereas birth is cause for celebration, death has become a dreaded and unspeakable issue to be avoided by every means possible in our modern society. Perhaps it is that death reminds us of our human vulnerability in spite of all our technical advances. We may be able to delay it, but we cannot escape it.

— Elisabeth Kübler-Ross

Despite amazing advances in medical science and technology, the mortality rate for human beings stands at a whopping 100 percent. It's a fact: All of us are going to die someday. Yet in the face of this statistical reality, we are often unprepared when death arrives. When death claims those we love, we struggle with our grief, seek comfort from relatives and friends, and cling to the accepted, society-approved ways to celebrate and memorialize a person's life — all while managing the unfamiliar, stressful tasks of funeral and burial arrangements.

Yet our modern burial customs often fall short of our

needs. The typical ceremony run by a funeral home — one that involves embalming and a casket burial in a traditional cemetery — not only can fail to provide a satisfying ritual for mourning, but it frequently leaves behind lasting financial and ecological burdens. Traditional burials can become very expensive, and they usually lead to environmental damage. Yet in the upheaval of the moment, we often make choices that are more elaborate and expensive than we want or need because we don't realize we have options: options to simplify, options to be more hands-on, options to go green. We've become convinced that parting with lots of money — as our final gift to someone that allows them to eternally rest in peace — is just the way it is and the way it's always been.

This isn't true. Throughout most of human history, burial practices have differed from what they are today, and despite appearances, modern American cemeteries are not tranquil green gardens. From the headstones to the caskets to the pesticide-treated lawns, they are instead increasingly toxic places whose soil is filled with chemicals and metals that are harmful to nature and to the living.

Not exactly ashes to ashes and dust to dust.

This doesn't have to be the case. What if our burial customs actually facilitated the "cycle of life," so that we sustained the environment rather than harmed it? What if our rituals were personal, heartfelt, community endeavors that didn't end in an expensive final bill that strained our resources? What if we planned ahead for our own eventual death, and so ensured that our burial makes a positive impact on our family and the environment even long after we are gone?

Death is a natural occurrence, and ideally the ways that we mourn and dispose of the dead should feel natural and support nature. Today, many people are trying to lessen the negative impact of human society on the environment in a multitude of ways: by supporting renewable energy, by driving hybrid or electric cars, by eating healthy foods, by promoting sustainable agriculture, by using their own cloth bags at the grocery store, and so on. Another area where we need to consider our impact on the planet is in how we handle the dead.

Green burial is a way of caring for our dead with the least possible environmental impact. It is a set of body preparations and burial practices that allow a body to decompose naturally in a site specifically set aside for this type of environmentally sound resting at peace. Meanwhile, hand in hand with green burials, home funerals are becoming more common, in which people create their own services and make their own end-of-life arrangements, rather than hiring the services of a mainstream funeral home.

Green burials and home funerals are not new ideas; they have been practiced for thousands of years and are still universally practiced in many countries around the world. While death can be a difficult subject, I hope that this book helps you plan for its eventuality. I hope it opens your eyes to all the choices that are available to you when it comes to funerals and burials. I hope it helps you see that it's possible to lower costs and lower impacts while still creating a beautiful send-off for the person who has passed.

Ultimately, that's the aim of green burial, to leave the

Earth a little better than it was before your loved one was placed into its gentle and natural embrace.

My First Green Burial

As a small child, I saw a lot of people die, and I attended their rosaries, visitations, funerals, and burials. I knew these people; they were my neighbors, church members, and even my family. My mother and grandparents, who lived with us, all died before I was ten years old. As I grew older, I learned to nurture friends when they had deaths to deal with, whether the deaths involved a grandmother or a gerbil.

As a young adult, it felt only natural to pursue mortuary science and become a funeral director. My first foray into the funeral industry was as the live-in night keeper in a hilly cemetery at age twenty-two. I received my funeral director's license in California first, and then I moved back to my home state of Oregon and passed the test there. After many years, I finally was able to own and operate my own funeral parlor.

I can truly attest that being a funeral director is less a job than a calling. I used to have a cherished reoccurring dream of being an angel in white. It made me feel beautiful, radiant, and most of all, at peace. I often feel that my life as a mortician bears a certain resemblance to the angel in white. I am giving myself to others, and in return, I am given life.

This is how I run my business. I know that death isn't a failure, a battle that has been lost. Conventional wisdom says we should tell someone we are sorry for their loss, and that we should look but not touch. But I have learned that people grieve in many different ways and that they are their most authentic selves during this process. Emotions come in waves, and it is hard to feel that an hour or two spent in the funeral home is intimate enough, is time enough to say goodbye. I've learned that whatever I can do to help people be more present in the process certainly aids in bereavement healing.

Yet about ten years back, my calling as an undertaker took on new meaning. My funeral parlor phone rang, and a woman asked if I could meet her and some friends at their favorite pub to discuss funeral arrangements for a woman named Wanda, who had just died. Wanda's friends were a close-knit group of gentle people. While filling out the death certificate, they were stumped as to why they weren't allowed to list Wanda's occupation as "Wanderer" and her industry as "the Earth." After all, that was how Wanda saw herself. Her friends came to see me because they felt they could only accurately honor Wanda the Wanderer by laying her to rest on the fifteen country acres where she lived in community with others, but they weren't sure how to go about doing that.

In fact, I wasn't certain this was legal, so I made some calls. The local zoning department confirmed that private land burials were allowed in Wanda's county, and they explained the regulations to me. I was stunned to find all this out...and excited. So, I lined up a backhoe, and by the next day, we were ready for the fitting ceremony.

Wanda had walked a green life, and now we would help her walk a green death.

The service was top-drawer, almost like the kind of party Wanda would have created if she were alive. Her friends and family played drums, chanted, and spoke of her kindness.

We all held hands to form a circle around her newly dug resting place and stood in silence as her three sons lowered her gently into the earth. Her tiny frame was cloaked with a quilt she had made as a teenager. Soon, the plain grave was covered with soil. We left a raised knoll of dirt on top to compensate for the settling that would happen over time. We used no grave marker, just native foliage. After a closing prayer, we feasted on fish caught down the way in the Clackamas River.

Wanda's family and friends conducted her funeral in their own way, and I could see how much comfort it gave them to be able to stay with her and take care of her body themselves. They were with her the whole process: from the time she died until the time she was buried. It was like in the old days, but I felt as if I had discovered something new. For once I didn't have the nagging feeling that the whole experience of burial was falling short for the mourners. I felt I'd been true to my calling as a funeral director to help a loving group of family and friends get what they needed from their send-off. Burial is the last thing you can do for someone, all of which makes green burial positively down-to-earth and uplifting.

After the burial, the family called to share their collective consciousness that Wanda wasn't isolated in her grave space. She had become one with the bionetwork that supported every plant and creature, and as she rested eternally in nature's embrace, life would now surround her.

Overview of This Guidebook

Green burial may seem like an avant-garde choice, but in the not-too-distant past, we would keep our recently deceased loved one at home, buy a casket from the local general store, prepare a resting space in the backyard or churchyard, and then conduct the burial ourselves with some simple reflection and quiet dignity. As you will learn in these pages, it is legal today to bury a loved one without an embalmed body, nor do you need to use a gasketed casket inside a protective grave liner. It's a myth that all bodies need to be embalmed before burial, and in most states, you aren't required to hire a funeral director. That said, burial rules and regulations vary by state and local laws, which is why planning ahead for a funeral, especially for a green burial, is so important, since it avoids unexpected legal problems during an already stressful time.

This book will guide you in that planning, while presenting you with the full range of options to consider. I've written this book as a simple, straightforward guide to green burial practices, one that shares all the tools and information you need to use more natural, sustainable methods. My hope is you will mark up this guidebook, bending page corners, and writing notes in the margins so this becomes your go-to green tool kit whenever you need it.

In part 1, I briefly discuss the topic of green burial in general. In chapter 1, I explore the environmental impacts of current burial practices and the funeral industry. In chapter 2, I look at various religious and social attitudes about death and burial, along with some of the different ways that people around the world currently practice green burial and hope to do so in the near future.

Meanwhile, part 2 is a step-by-step guide to planning your own green burial and conducting your own home funeral. You might say, green burials come in a vast spectrum of shades. What's right for you really depends, and what's best in each particular situation will certainly vary. You may wish to use a funeral home and the cemetery where the rest of your family is buried, but still conduct the greenest burial possible, or you may want to build your own casket, dig a backyard grave, and handle the body yourself. This book will help you in both these situations, as well as many more.

Green burials and home funerals are meant to reflect the unique expression and needs of the people involved. There is no "standard format," and you will need to decide for yourself what works and what's important. On the other hand, there are full-service green funeral homes that can assist you, and there are trained professionals who can act as guides throughout your journey. With green burials, you are in charge, but you don't have to do it alone.

Meanwhile, throughout this book, you will find two types of sidebars: "Tips" provide just that, nitty-gritty details that I've spent years learning so you don't have to. The other, "Tales from the Grave," shares unusual burial facts and traditions from around the globe, since the dead have more stories than a library. At the end of the book are further resources, endnotes, and an index.

Ultimately, my fervent hope is that the tools and techniques you learn here will provide the practical, logistical, and spiritual support you need to know the joys and sorrows of laying your loved one to rest in your own way, in the manner that is most meaningful and important to you. I certainly hope that includes a range of green or environmentally friendly practices. But whatever you choose to do,

I would be remiss not to acknowledge the obvious: Death is hard, and we are rarely prepared for it. In the moment, faced with the reality of death, sometimes all our planning goes out the window, and we have to do whatever we have to do to take care of ourselves and others. Emotions can be raw and unexpected, and we may not be able to follow through on everything we mean to. That's okay. Life isn't perfect, and neither is death, which is one reason why people are sometimes grateful to hand funeral planning over to professionals.

Just know that you don't have to. The Funeral Consumers Alliance has always touted, "Losing a loved one is hard. Planning a funeral shouldn't be." That's certainly true, so long as you plan ahead — and *The Green Burial Guidebook* is here to help!

Part

I

WHAT IS GREEN BURIAL?

Chapter I

GREEN BURIAL, THE FUNERAL INDUSTRY, AND THE ENVIRONMENT

G reen or natural burials have existed since the beginning of time. For most of human history, when the dead were buried (and not disposed of by other means), the body was wrapped in a shroud or perhaps placed in a simple wooden box, and then the deceased was lowered into a hole, covered with dirt, and returned to the earth. While mummification and embalming were known and practiced in Egypt, China, and other civilizations thousands of years ago, this was not the common practice for the clear majority of people.

Further, up until the last one hundred years or so, people all over the globe have tended to their deceased loved ones in their own households, with their own hands, and with their own time and love. Yet today, Americans seem more comfortable with handing over the steps of caring for their dead to licensed morticians in funeral parlors. Over time, our society has dealt with death less and less openly, until we arrived at where we are now, largely ignorant of our options and our rights throughout the whole procedure.

This chapter defines green burials and home funerals, and then it discusses the environmental problems with current burial practices.

What Are Green Burials and Home Funerals?

In the most familiar definition, a green burial means a person is buried in a container that can decompose, along with their human remains, and return to the soil. Ideally, all aspects of a green burial are as organic as possible. The body is not filled with embalming chemicals, and it is placed in the earth without vaults or nonbiodegradable caskets. The end goal of green burial is that nothing is used that doesn't help replenish the soil.

In the United States, some traditional cemeteries will accommodate burial without the use of a vault or casket liner in their grave plots. However, there are also dedicated green cemeteries and "green burial sites that also facilitate ecological restoration and landscape-level conservation," writes scholar Tanja Schade. These burial spaces feature sustainable landscaping and natural markers as headstones, and they may preserve land where native plants and animal life flourish.

Meanwhile, home funerals are a return to traditional ways, in the same manner that green burials are a return to traditional burial practices. A home funeral can be a healing, comforting experience for the loved ones affected by a loss.

A home funeral can include all of the elements of a customary funeral, but, to quote the *NBC News* report "More Families Are Bringing Funerals Home," a home funeral is "an intimate experience: friends or family members might help wash and dress the body, build or decorate a casket, plan a memorial service, or accompany the deceased to the burial site or crematory."

The website Seven Ponds (see Resources) promotes green burials and home funerals and emphasizes the many options available: "You can also find a funeral home, with a refrigeration unit, willing to refrigerate and transport the body, without embalming it. A funeral may be held at home before the body is transported to the burial site. Alternatively, a memorial service or life celebration may be held long after the body is buried."

What Do Green Burials Look Like?

I feel quite honored to have been able to help many families green the ceremonies and burials for their loved ones. And no two have really been the same, as we are all such unique and special people. I have arranged for people to transport their deceased family members in all sorts of vehicles, have helped people choose the perfect burial site on private property, and have witnessed communities joining together in creative ways to honor a member who has died.

In Portland in 2010, a woman named Alyce was dying from ovarian cancer. About a month before she died, her best friend, Diane, came into my funeral home to make plans and figure out how she could create a funeral that best aligned with her tender-hearted friend's spirit. We made a plan: Once she died, Alyce would stay in her home. We figured out which cemetery she would be transported to and by whom. I assisted Diane with assembling her team of helpers and assigning jobs.

Alyce was also involved in this planning, and she was very thoughtful about what she wanted and how it might unfold. Diane visited George Cemetery in Estacada, Oregon, and chose the burial space. She also had ready Alyce's oatmeal-hued, organic cotton dress, which Alyce wanted to be dressed in for her final journey to the cemetery. For the burial, Alyce was also wrapped in a natural blanket that shrouded her small frame, and she was placed onto a pine board for easier carrying — from the home, into the back of the station wagon, and to the gravesite.

Once at the cemetery, Alyce's friends gently lowered her into the ground and shared some words. In particular, someone spoke about how Alyce had always wanted to become a tree, and now that dream was going to come true.

∞

As part of their home funeral for their father, three brothers — Bill, Ralph, and Jim — sat quietly on a wooden deck hanging off the side of the family's old farmhouse. Nearby, a cherry tree extended its gangly limbs full of righteous red fruit, which reached all the way to the deck. After a prayer, the brothers were ready to lay their father to rest about twenty feet away, a sweet space where the cherry branches would extend over the grave, providing shelter always, even during the winter when there were no leaves and no fruit. Of course, the tree would also shade their father in the summer.

At the gravesite, a long piece of muslin cloth was used to lower the body down into the grave, and then the "pallbearers" (those holding the cloth, since there was no casket) let the cloth go, so it fell across the shrouded body. The bottom of the grave had been lined with pine boughs, and now more were thrown over the body. The boughs were symbolic, but they also help hasten decomposition. If the brothers had used a biodegradable coffin or placed their father on a board intended to be buried with him, ropes would have been used to lower him. Instead, the "ropes" or lowering cords were sewn directly into the burial wrap.

Finally, the three brothers all moved shovelfuls of dirt to cover their beloved father's resting space, and they laughed over and shared childhood memories with everyone at the ceremony.

The Most Important Aspects of a Green Burial

There are lots of ways to make a burial more environmentally friendly, but a few components are the most important for creating a true green burial. Part 2 discusses all these options in more detail.

Don't Use a Decorative Casket

The typical casket used today is not made to be biodegradable; it's made for preservation. Modern burial boxes are manufactured from reinforced steel or shellacked hardwoods, then embellished with metals, handles, and ornamentation. All that metal, lacquer, and toxic glue is certainly no good for the environment.

If you decide you want a casket, opt for a basic wooden casket, like a plain pine box, or one made from other natural materials: bamboo, sea grass, banana leaves, and even willow branches. Earth-friendly caskets are fully biodegradable. They will break down to nothing, and they shouldn't have any traces of metal, toxic glue, plastic, or varnish.

However, you don't need to use a casket at all. A deceased person can easily be wrapped in a favorite nonbleached or dyed cloth, blanket, or tapestry, and several types of commercially made burial shrouds and wraps are now sold. For more on all these types of green burial containers, see chapter 7.

Don't Use a Burial Vault or Grave Liner

A burial vault — also referred to as a grave box, casket liner, or outer burial container — is a container made from concrete or polypropylene, and it is used to surround the casket for maximum preservation and to prevent the grave from collapsing over time. Green cemeteries prohibit them entirely, and traditional cemeteries are beginning to forgo their obligatory inclusion. A green burial should be designed to allow the body to naturally return to the earth at the fastest rate possible. By not using a vault, the process happens much more quickly.

Decline Embalming

Embalming fluid contains formaldehyde, a likely carcinogen that is hazardous to the environment as well as to the embalmer. Forgoing standard embalming doesn't necessarily mean that a funeral must happen more quickly: Alternatives do exist for preserving a body for a moderate period, such as "green embalming" techniques as well as good old-fashioned refrigeration and dry ice. If you are using a funeral home, they will be able to assist with standard refrigeration, but if you are handling the body yourself, you will need some instruction; see chapter 8 for more on this.

However, don't let the idea of an unpreserved body gross you out. The Centers for Disease Control and Prevention makes it clear that the average dead body is neither dangerous nor contagious. Our society has developed a number of myths and misconceptions about dead bodies that I hope this book will help dispel.

Use a Green Burial Site

Ideally, to ensure an eco-friendly burial, choose a fully natural burial ground whose sole purpose is eco-conservation. Another great choice is a hybrid or low-impact green cemetery, a burial area that has adopted environmental practices but also allows for traditional graves. Or, if the law allows and the land is available, consider a backyard burial. See chapter 6 for more on this. A backyard burial takes some extra planning, and some extra work, but it may be the greenest way to say goodbye.

Wood engraving of the process of embalming, circa 1885
(Art credit: New York Public Library)

A Brief History of Modern Burial Practices

Up until 150 years ago, most burials were inherently green, the focus being the return of the body to the earth. When a family member passed away, the steps were modest: Bathe, prepare, and place the body in a humble wood box. For a short time, display the body at home for neighbor visits, and then bury the coffin in a family plot on the family farm or in a small-town or church cemetery.

But during the Civil War, soldiers were killed in such multitudes that their bodies couldn't be disposed of in a timely fashion. As Suzanne Kelly writes in *Greening Death*: "Newly trained civilian medical professionals were called into action, and over four years' time, as many as forty thousand bodies were embalmed. For families who wanted it, and who could also afford it, bodies were shipped back home for burial." By replacing the body's natural fluids with formal-dehyde and other chemicals, a body could be restored, preserved for some time, and transported long distances.

TALES FROM THE GRAVE

After President Lincoln was assassinated, the way his body was handled seemed very foreign to American citizens at the time. Lincoln's body was sent by train from Washington, DC, to Springfield, Illinois, making several stops along the way for the mourning nation to pay their respects. Brand-new embalming methods helped preserve the late president so that he did not start decomposing during his long travels and in front of all his admirers.

Embalming became a profitable service industry, and the business of funeral directing was born. Soon, it became standard practice to quickly whisk a dead body out of the home and to a funeral parlor, where the deceased was restored to look as lifelike as possible. After an expansive and expensive memorialization period, the undertaker buried the body in a fancy casket in a manicured graveyard. The coffin was placed inside a concrete vault, which prevented the coffin from collapsing and the ground from sinking. This uneven ground made mowing at cemeteries problematic, and it also reminded living visitors of the unpleasant fact of dead bodies beneath the earth. Each new wrinkle in funeral practice seemed designed to add to the illusion of the perpetual preservation of the cadaver.

Today, as Jessica Mitford illuminated in her 1963 best-seller *The American Way of Death*, Americans tend to be very squeamish around death, and they prefer that burial arrangements are handled at a funeral parlor by trained people who know what they are doing, even if it costs a fortune. Mitford delighted in saying that the funeral industry "successfully turned the tables in recent years to perpetuate a huge, macabre and expensive practical joke on the American public."

We like neat. Clean. Not to get our hands too dirty. Those of us left behind do all we can to remember and honor the deceased as they were when they were living, and conversely, we try to hide all signs that they are now dead. Yet the consequences of this attitude and of these burial practices have led to a host of environmental problems that also remain largely unseen and unacknowledged.

TALES FROM THE GRAVE

How squeamish are Americans about death? We are the country that, during the eighteenth and nineteenth centuries, created the safety coffin — which included a bell to ring that would alert graveyard workers if the unfortunate soul inside was being buried alive.

The Environmental Impacts of Traditional Burials

Worldwide, official estimates are that more than 50 million people pass away each year, which includes almost 3 million people in the United States. How these people are buried certainly makes a difference to nature and the environment.

Current practices typically bury lots of bad things in the ground, and this is having negative environmental impacts. "The typical ten-acre swath of cemetery ground," notes Mark Harris in his 2007 book *Grave Matters*, "contains enough coffin wood to construct more than forty homes, nine hundred-plus tons of casket steel, and another twenty thousand tons of vault concrete. To that add a volume of embalming fluid sufficient to fill a small backyard swimming pool and untold gallons of pesticide and weed killer to keep the graveyard preternaturally green. Like the contents of any landfill, the embalmed body's toxic cache escapes its host and eventually leaches into the environment, tainting surrounding soil and ground waters. Cemeteries bear the chemical legacy of their embalmed dead, and well after their graves have been closed."

Katrina Spade, founder of Recompose, writes that conventional burials contribute to emissions by several means. "Although embalming slows the decomposition process, it does not stop it completely. In the weeks and months following a conventional burial, bodies slowly decompose anaerobically, and this lack of oxygen creates methane, a particularly powerful greenhouse gas." Even more emissions occur during the construction of traditional caskets and grave liners. Then, beautifully manicured cemeteries don't happen with just water, seed, and sunlight. Gallons of pesticides and fuel must be used to weed, mow, and preserve the grass.

To quantify these impacts with slightly different numbers, here are some statistics provided by Mary Woodsen, founding president of Greensprings Natural Cemetery near Ithaca, New York, and science writer at Cornell University. According to her, each year conventional funeral and burial practices in the United States result in the use of

- 4.3 million gallons of embalming fluid, which contains formaldehyde, a known carcinogen;
- 1.6 million tons of concrete, from burial vaults; and
- 20 million board feet of hardwood for caskets.

Or, according to Joe Sehee, founder of the Green Burial Council, each year "we bury enough embalming fluid to fill eight Olympic-sized swimming pools, enough metal to build the Golden Gate Bridge, and so much reinforced concrete in burial vaults that we could build a two-lane highway from New York to Detroit."

Cremation: Ashes to Ashes Doesn't Always Mean Green

After the 1963 publication of Jessica Mitford's bestselling book *The American Way of Death,* cremation was embraced by many as the better ecological alternative to traditional burial, and cremation experienced a meteoric increase. The main concern was space: Since cremated remains take up no space, if they are scattered, or very little space, if they are preserved in an urn, this saves the land for the living.

According to a 2016 *Time* magazine report, only about 10 percent of people in the United States chose cremation in 1980, but it's risen steadily ever since, and today, about 49 percent of people choose cremation versus 45 percent who choose traditional burial. There are several reasons for this:

- Cremation is much less expensive than modern burial, by 50 percent or more.
- Cremation requires little planning, either before or after death.
- Remains are portable, so they may be placed almost anywhere, and they can be dispersed in places that are meaningful.

While cremation remains a better ecological choice than modern burial, cremation is not considered a genuine environmental alternative for a few reasons. The main reason is because of the energy it takes. Typically, cremation ovens use fossil fuels, and they must maintain a temperature of 1,800 degrees Fahrenheit for more than two hours, which burns a lot of fuel. Cremation emits mercury and other elements into the air and water, plus it produces 250 pounds of carbon dioxide. The United Nations estimates that crematoriums contribute up to 0.2 percent of the annual global emission of greenhouse gases, and cremation adds to heavy metal particulates in air pollution.

In addition, cremation ashes — sometimes called cremains — are not themselves "green." Cremation ashes are primarily tricalcium phosphate with small amounts of other minerals and salts unique to each body. Human ashes are comprised of different elements depending on what a person's body contained, which depends on their nutrition and their lifetime exposure to heavy metals and chemicals. This is exactly why you should never dig a hole, dump cremation ashes in it, and plant a tree on top of them. Cremation ashes are not like fertilizer. Carbon, nitrogen, and all the usable nutrients for plant growth are burned away, disappearing into the atmosphere. In addition, if you plant a tree or foliage over cremains, consult local experts and choose species that are native to the region.

> TIP: If you want to scatter cremains or bury them, follow the advice of Gail Rubin and Susan Fraser, who wrote *Celebrating Life*: "Incorporate the ashes lightly into the soil. This way, the ashes may contribute to the environment by providing nutrients for flowers and other plants. This process is known as raking." Raking allows the cremated remains to commingle as gently as possible with soil, so that plant life isn't harmed by the highly concentrated pH levels of cremains.

In other words, while cremation may save ground space, this isn't an environmentally friendly send-off. Ever wonder why, when human cremains are scattered at sea, most states require this to be done at least three miles off the coastline? Much of the time, when cremains are scattered, they remain visible and do not decompose as readily as once thought. And if the remains haven't been properly pulverized — processed in a machine to become the same texture as ash or sand — then bone fragments and other small chunks can take quite a while to biodegrade naturally.

Chapter 2

GREEN BURIAL PRACTICES

Yesterday, Today, and Tomorrow

Though the topic of death has long been unpleasant in our culture, it is an essential part of life. In many religions and cultures around the world, it is accepted, acknowledged, and even celebrated. Until we learn to deal with death justly and embrace it, we are not living as our paramount selves. This includes taking an authentic look at how we perform our funerals and burials, as well as the ways other cultures handle these rituals.

This chapter briefly surveys some of these attitudes and alternative green burial practices: those in the past, those in other cultures, and those that may one day reshape our burial customs entirely.

Traditional Religions and Burial Rituals

In Genesis 3:19, the Bible says, "For dust thou art, and unto dust shalt thou return."

Many religions ask us to live modestly, and that principle extends to death. The Catholic Church is becoming a leading religious force reclaiming the ancient, green methods of burial, since it supports the doctrine of resurrection. In addition, Pope Francis has expressed a deep love of nature and a very clear stance on consumerism, stating that all people have a responsibility to care for our Earth.

The Catholic Church is a large supporter of green burial, which is a method of laying a human body to rest with rebirth in mind. Catholics believe that the body will one day be reunited with its soul for eternal life, and in the words of Maureen McGuinness, family service manager of upstate New York's Most Holy Redeemer Cemetery, green burial "is a way for families to talk about resurrection."

The church supports older traditions. According to Maria Margiotta, "Before the development of chemical embalming, metal-lined caskets, or cement burial vaults, there was simply a shroud and a hole in the ground...a burial tradition that humankind embraced for thousands of years." Father Charles Morris — who oversees Mount Carmel Cemetery in Wyandotte, Michigan, the first US Catholic cemetery to offer a green burial option — has said, "While some may regard this form of burial as odd, remember that Jesus was laid to rest in a shroud, without embalming or a burial vault. This has been the way Christians have honored their loved ones throughout most of the Church's two thousand years."

The Jewish religion has also always practiced natural burials. Jewish customs align with the steps it takes to carry out a traditional green burial. The body is bathed by members of the faith and wrapped in a natural sheet. A natural wood casket encases the body, and the burial takes place in a short amount of time. According to the website Funeralwise, "Jewish funeral traditions require only the use of a simple casket. This practice serves as affirmation that everyone is equal in death."

Traditional Islamic burial practice states that the deceased loved one should be handled and ritually cleansed by a member of the same sex (and specifically in the direction of head to toe). The body is then lovingly laid to resemble a sleeping position, wrapped in perfumed white cloth, and placed directly into the ground in order to become one with the earth.

Scene of a Native American Burial

Native American burial, raised platform with body in field, 1910 (Photo credit: Museum of Photographic Arts Collection)

Native American traditions hold that the natural world is truly revered. Many religious ceremonies are tied to a specific location, and to harm that sacred space would be contrary to Native American beliefs. Because of this, Native American funeral practices have always been eco-friendly.

I had the honor to serve as funeral director for a Native American burial in the fall of 2011, when we laid to rest Chayton Lootah, also known as Hawk-That-Is-Red. At sunset, Chayton's father beat out a steady rhythm on his hand drum, which his grandmother had painted with images of the evening sky, while the rest of us completed a rock medicine wheel to honor Chayton's life. At this point, it was perfectly lovely to step back from my role of director to participate with the others.

Medicine wheels, which vary in size and mostly are circles of boulders or rocks, were once always built on sacred sites. The sites were often at the intersection of rivers, on mountaintops, or in the center of plains between mountain and rivers. The deceased were placed on a scaffold, along with their possessions. Mounds were built for burial, and bodies weren't embalmed. Grieving family and friends observed a four-day wake, and food was set out on the scaffolding.

As we constructed our medicine wheel of stone and branches, we could feel the energy flowing: from the intersections of energy lines related to churches and sacred sites, and from ourselves, as we lay the dearly departed Chayton to rest.

After the incense was lit, we set off in all directions to find the correct magical twig. Someone finally found a willow branch. It was pliable, so we bent the twig into a circle and bound it closed, then we tied a piece of ribbon from north to south across it and then tied another piece from east to west, dividing the circle of willow into four equal parts. In the middle, where the two ribbons crossed, we placed the prongs of a sheep and a poem Chayton wrote shortly before his death.

People desiring green burials are often motivated by strong spiritual and/or philosophical beliefs and motivations. A well-known Native American chant translates as, "The Earth is our mother; we must take care of her." This belief is expressed by many religious faiths and by those of no religious faith. It's a philosophy and sense of personal responsibility that can motivate anyone to choose natural or green burial.

TALES FROM THE GRAVE

If you visit the Philippines, head to the northern city of Sagada to view the amazing cliff of hanging coffins. In this two-thousand-year-old tradition, the elderly carve their own coffins out of hollowed logs (or get help making one). Then, once deceased, the person is placed inside the coffin (it's a tight fit and sometimes bones need to be broken), and the coffins are hung from the cliff face.

The tradition itself is dying out, though it is supposedly still practiced. It's speculated that the hanging coffins were originally used to prevent bodies from being taken by animals or simply because the higher your coffin, the higher your spirit would rise eternally.

TALES FROM THE GRAVE

In the high mountains of Tibet, with hard ground and little wood, the tradition of "sky burials" is as natural as it gets: a dead body is left exposed on a flat rock so that vultures, large birds, and animals will eat it in its entirety. This method of disposition remains common in Tibet, since Tibetan Buddhism regards a dead body as an "empty vessel" that doesn't need preservation. The exact ritual varies (and at times, cost seems to be a factor), but it can involve helper monks who cut the body into pieces, break up bones, and smash any remains that vultures leave behind into a pulp that is left for other birds.

The Return of Green Cemeteries

The natural burial movement gained steam in the early 1990s, and green burial grounds soon followed. One of the first was in England. Ken West, who was the bereavement services manager of the Carlisle municipal cemetery, decided to reserve a part of the cemetery for green burial. At that time, his main concern was the poor British economy. It was a daunting task to try to improve the cemetery without much money, and offering low-budget green burial options proved to be fiscally and environmentally sound.

In the United States, one of the first natural burial grounds was Ramsey Creek Preserve, which opened in 1996 in western South Carolina. Ramsey Creek Preserve provides burial spaces among thirty-three acres of woodlands and open fields, in which the soothing sound of flowing water is constant.

Since then, green cemeteries have grown exponentially. In 2012, the United Kingdom had more than 250 green burial sites, and as of 2017, the United States had at least 153 official green cemeteries.

Now, with the baby boomer generation (those born between 1946 and 1964) slowly starting to check out of the world, we will surely see an increase in green burials and green cemeteries. After all, the baby boomer generation was the first green generation: They organized Earth Day and helped birth the modern environmental movement. This eco-conscious age group will most likely redefine our burial traditions as well, one burial at a time, with each person sharing their own compelling story. Many in this generation embraced the idea of walking gently on this Earth, so it is only natural they will continue that trend in death.

Death Cafes: A Modern, Secular Movement

More recently, along with the green burial movement, has been the rise of Death Cafes. These are informal gatherings of people with a curiosity about and a desire to discuss death. There is no agenda for these meetings, other than to discuss death, and hearing and sharing everyone's perspective is encouraged. To quote the official website: "At a Death Cafe, people, often strangers, gather to eat cake, drink tea, and discuss death. Our objective is 'to increase awareness of death with a view to helping people make the most of their (finite) lives.'"

Death Cafes began in England in 2011 and have since spread throughout the world. In particular, it has become a very large movement in the Pacific Northwest, where people feel supported to have this resource. These meetings can be hosted by anyone, anywhere. The goal is simply to encourage the general public, and anyone who attends, to feel safe sharing their opinions, asking questions, and hearing other perspectives on death, dying, last rites, funeral practices, and so on. Particularly for anyone who has never had the misfortune (or not!) to attend a funeral, a wake, a burial, or any sort of ceremony for the dead, Death Cafes can be a great way to explore your own thoughts and feelings.

Green Burials of the Famous

Celebrities are known for making their burials as big and bright as their Hollywood star. It is exciting to me every time I see a famous person (movie star or not) choose a natural burial. The following are examples of famous people who opted for a green burial:

In 2016, country singer Joey Feek, from the married country duo Joey + Rory, died from cervical cancer. A space was prepared for her burial on the family farm in Pottsville, Tennessee. As quoted in *People* magazine, Rory wrote that "a team of mules carried Joey's simple wooden box in an 1800's wagon with six of Joey's favorite 'cowboys' by her side."

In 2010, British actress Lynn Redgrave's body was laid to rest in a woven bamboo casket, which was covered with flowers. Many caskets thatched together from sustainable materials are secured with a series of wooden dowels, which fit through small rope loops. Lynn and her eco-casket had their final interment in a rural cemetery in Lithgow, Connecticut. Her brother, Corin, had died just one month prior to Lynn and was buried in a very similar casket.

According to reports on CNN, television legend Andy Griffith was buried less than five hours after he died, with no embalming and in a natural casket. At the request of his family, his body was lowered into a grave on his family property on Roanoke Island in North Carolina, his home state.

Civil rights leader and founder of the United Farm Workers (UFW), Cesar Chavez died on April 23, 1993. Fifty thousand mourners made a pilgrimage to watch him pass by when he was brought to Delano, California, for burial. As might be expected, his body was carried in a simple, humble pine box, made by his brother, that was specified by Chavez before he died.

Funeral Pyres: Crestone End-of-Life Project

How do you turn cremation into a genuine green burial? By being cremated in an open-air funeral pyre, which is more carbon neutral because it burns wood, not gas or propane. If the body is not embalmed, the process is greener still. This type of cremation remains very rare, and funerary and cremation industry officials I've spoken to say they know of only one place in the United States that conducts open-air cremations for people regardless of religion.

That's the Crestone Cemetery and Natural Burial Ground in Colorado (see Resources). The land is owned and administered by the town of Crestone and offers a spectacular view of the adjacent Sangre de Cristo Mountains. Six acres are fenced and platted with twenty-by-twenty-foot lots and five-foot aisles. Burial regulations are minimal, with no restrictions or requirements regarding caskets, embalming, vaults, or decorations. While all types of burials are allowed, including traditional ones, there have been no burials using concrete vaults.

"Ancient Vikings lit funeral pyres to honor their dead, and it is accepted practice among Buddhist and Hindu religions," stated Ivan Moreno in a 2011 Associated Press report, "but the practice is largely taboo in the United States."

Besides Crestone, funeral pyres in the United States are only conducted by religious groups, such as a Buddhist temple in nearby Red Feather Lakes, and these burials are available only to members. Typically, the funeral pyre is similar to a fire pit at a campground, only larger. The body is wrapped in a plain cloth shroud, and at Red Feather Lakes, juniper logs and branches are used for kindling. Family members are offered the choice to light the funeral pyre themselves with a torch. According to the Associated Press story, "Volunteers counsel grieving family, help arrange the deceased to repose at home before the cremation, and prepare the hearth with kindling the day before the ceremony."

TALES FROM THE GRAVE

They are formally known as "forensic anthropology research facilities," but these outdoor areas are more commonly known as "body farms." At body farms, dead bodies are tracked as they move through the various stages of decomposition. Seven body farms currently operate in the United States. The first body farm broke ground in the 1970s and was created by Dr. William Bass, a forensic anthropologist, who wanted to study human decomposition to solve crimes.

Like body donation, this is "green burial" in the name of science and education.

Green Burials of Tomorrow

Not only will life look a lot different in the future, but death will, too. Here are four techniques that may define the green burials of tomorrow, and some of them are available today!

Upright or Vertical Burials

Many people who choose cremation over traditional burial do so because they don't want to take up so much space after death, in addition to the lower cost of cremation — about $2,000 compared to about $7,000 for a conventional burial — and other environmental reasons.

But what if you were buried upright? In Australia (and a few other places), vertical burials are being adopted as a green approach to traditional burial. In a cemetery near Melbourne, the deceased are placed in biodegradable shrouds and buried in cylindrical holes, in a feet-first position. This method allows for twice as many burial spaces as a typical cemetery, and since no embalming or expensive casket is used, it is truly a green burial.

I can see how a vertical burial kind of ruins the image of eternal rest. But I like to think being interred in an upright orientation would make one much more aerodynamic, making it easier to float to heaven more quickly.

Freeze-Dried Cadavers

Adapting a concept that has been applied to food but not people, Swedish biologist Susanne Wiigh-Mäsak has been developing a method of green burial that uses freeze-drying. Her company is called Promessa, which is derived from the Italian word for "promise," and it's successfully tested the process. A dead body is placed in liquid nitrogen, which removes the water from the body, effectively freeze-drying it, and then vibrations disintegrate the body into fine particles, which are sealed inside a biodegradable coffin and buried in a shallow grave. In under a year, the remains become compost or nutrient-rich soil. Wiigh-Mäsak hopes that this becomes yet one more environmentally friendly way to dispose of human remains.

Capsula Mundi

Based in Italy, Capsula Mundi is another green burial concept that's still being developed and tested. The idea is that the deceased will be placed in a fetal position inside an organic, egg-shaped pod, which will then be buried with a tree planted on top of it. Over time, this will create a burial forest rather than a burial ground.

The Capsula Mundi pods will be entirely organic and will break down easily, allowing the body to decompose naturally and infuse the soil with natural nutrients. While no bodies have been used yet, they are testing the technique using cremation ashes. Of course, the resulting tree replaces the headstone, making a natural marker, and people could choose the species of tree they prefer, though designers Anna Citelli and Raoul Bretzel note that it would be best to choose species indigenous to the local ecosystem, since they would adapt and grow best.

Recompose

Recompose is the brainchild of Washington State's Katrina Spade, and it is yet another technique for turning human remains into nutrient-rich earth, so that death supports life and not the other way around. Spade has designed a system that will function not unlike a typical composting container: Bodies will be placed on a bed of "biological remnants," such as wood chips and straw. In about a month, the bodies and wood chips will steadily decompose and turn into soil, which will be removed and used by farmers and others. Spade calls this process "recomposition," and the first composting facility, based in Seattle, is on target to be a reality by 2023.

Spade imagines that the building will resemble a chapel or sanctuary, so that the entire process for families wouldn't be unlike a traditional funeral service. The life of their loved one will be celebrated, and everyone will participate in the process during what she calls the "laying in" ceremony.

Part

2

A GUIDE TO
GREEN BURIALS

Chapter 3

MAKING A PLAN

Green Burials and Home Funerals

The reality is that you will grieve forever. You will not "get over" the loss of a loved one; you will learn to live with it. You will heal and you will rebuild yourself around the loss you have suffered. You will be whole again but you will never be the same. Nor should you be the same nor would you want to. Death is but a transition from this life to another existence where there is no more pain and anguish. All the bitterness and disagreements will vanish, and the only thing that lives forever is love.

— Elisabeth Kübler-Ross, *On Grief and Grieving*

We all know that we need to plan ahead for our own death and for the deaths of our loved ones. But these are hard things to consider, and hard conversations to have, and we often put them off. A recent survey by the Conversation Project confirms what I've encountered myself: "While more than nine in ten Americans think it's important to talk about their own and their loved ones' wishes for end-of-life care, less than three in ten have actually held these sorts of discussions."

Don't be part of the 70 percent. Consider what you want, or what others want, for end-of-life care and burial arrangements, and discuss these with your family and friends. Share your preferences and your motivations for choosing them. To help others take care of you in the way you want when you're gone, clearly blueprint your final wishes. Write down how you want your body handled, how you would like to be celebrated, and the type of disposition you prefer. The advance directives part of your will is a good place to designate a person to carry out your wishes.

That said, I want to begin with a gentle note of caution: Sometimes your vision cannot be carried out. Time, or even weather, may not cooperate. There can be all kinds of stumbling blocks. By the time of your passing, the members of your assembled team may not be physically or emotionally able to follow through, your loved ones may disagree over what's best, or your well-choreographed ceremony may be too complicated, and so on. As you plan, anticipate this and build flexibility into your wishes. This gives yourself and others a grand gift, since it allows plans to be adapted while still fulfilling your wishes.

In this chapter, I will help you take the first steps in planning. I discuss what you should consider, costs to anticipate, and making a "funeral wish list." However, what makes considering these details so difficult, and why people often put them off, is the bigger questions they imply. They ask us to undertake a life review. How do we want to make peace with our family and the universe, and depart this world, with the utmost love and dignity? We have to consider this and let our wishes be known. Not only do we want a ceremony that aligns with our personality, or with the personality of a loved one, but we should consider how that ceremony will give people a quality opportunity to express their love and appreciation as a community.

When it comes to green burials and home funerals, it's even more important to make sure the people close to you understand your preferences and reasons. Unless you tell them, they may think it doesn't matter, or that you prefer a more traditional burial, using a typical casket, tombstone, embalming, and regular cemetery. Be prepared to answer any curious questions and explain the differences of natural burial. Perhaps even have resources ready, like websites, where people can learn more.

Ultimately, by choosing a natural or green burial, and providing clear instructions, you release your loved ones of the anguish that comes with having to make complicated, and often costly, decisions after your passing.

TALES FROM THE GRAVE

Traditionally, the Irish celebrate the deceased at home with an overnight vigil and party. Drinking and eating are encouraged, but grieving is not, since they believe that the person's soul is journeying happily to the next life. According to the website Nerdy Gaga: "Some Irish put a wooden plate on top of the deceased's chest with some amount of soil and salt. The soil symbolizes as 'the body will return into dusts,' and the salt symbolizes the soul that will not decay."

What Is Your Vision?

When I talk with families at my funeral home, I find people are increasingly interested in burials and funerals that are more environmentally and spiritually satisfying. Few in America currently care for their dead at home, but the number is increasing as people seek more intimacy and human connection with after-death-care details. Remember, green burials and home funerals are not new ideas. They are the oldest and most natural form of interment. Back in the day, the body was always kept at home, and family members oversaw the final plans.

What is your vision? What would be personally satisfying and feel right to you? What directives do you want to leave your survivors?

As you read this book, consider every aspect of green burials and home funerals, and keep a list of what's important to you. After your death, how do you want your body handled? Would you want it washed, dressed, and handled with grand kindness by a loved one? Would you like to assign "cadaver custodians" to wrap your body in a shroud, perhaps from a lovely tapestry that has hung on your wall for years? Would you prefer being placed in an organic cocoon made of banana leaves or thatched straw? Would you want your favorite music playing during these preparations?

Would you feel comforted to know your freshly clean body will be escorted by people you know and trust to a natural burial ground, a gorgeous, green pasture of flowers and trees? What sort of grave would you prefer, and how would you want to be placed in it: by certain people or in certain ways that reflect the refinement and care you desire? Are there aspects of the ceremony you'd like to specify? In what way do you want to be returned to the earth, so that in death you nourish the land and the loved ones you've left behind?

What would feel natural as friends come to visit your resting space? Would you want a tree to mark your grave, or would you prefer grasslands to cover you, with no marker at all? As the roots of these gifts of nature stretch down through the soil into your body, do you like the idea that you will rise up and live again to experience the phenomenon of living in the glory of the world? Does it make you smile to think of your visitors marveling at the fruitfulness of your body and praising you for the richness you have added to the planet?

It's as important to think of spiritual questions as practical ones. For help with both, you can also seek out a funeral home that offers or will help plan a green funeral or burial. All funeral homes are legally obligated to help you plan and execute a natural burial, so see what your local funeral director knows about green funeral options. If you talk to someone who just stares blankly back at you, keep looking. Some funeral homes have already adopted green practices in their preparation and burial techniques, making it much easier for you to plan a green burial. Plus, certified green funeral homes are becoming more prevalent. Visit the Green Burial Council (see Resources), which certifies green funeral homes and maintains a list of providers on their website. You may find great options in your area.

Set aside a quiet hour or two to think about your death and what you want for your burial arrangements. Think about how you want your funeral to look and feel for those who will gather in your honor. If you don't, your family will have to guess at a time when emotions will be running high. I have seen siblings fall out arguing over what photo to use on the front of the funeral program.

By writing out your after-care suggestions, your loved ones will hopefully feel less anxiety. We can't control how others grieve, but we can express what we want, which will give others permission to celebrate our life by fulfilling our wishes. This may help others cope with their sense of loss and provide a channel for mourning.

TIP: It's simple: If you want to be eco-friendlier, think less extravagantly. Kindness toward the Earth usually means doing less, and this attitude can be adapted to all facets of life, including death.

How Much Does a Green Burial Cost?

There isn't a standard cost for a green burial, since so many aspects of a modern funeral and burial can be either omitted or done yourself. Typically, green burials are less expensive than modern burials, and in some cases, they can be significantly less expensive. The difference usually depends on how much work you intend to do yourself and the cost of the materials and services you use.

An average estimate of a modern funeral and burial in the United States is anywhere from $6,000 to $10,000, depending on the specific goods and services you choose. Just like anything in life, you can choose the high-end model with all the extras, or you can pick the stripped-down floor model. Natural burial only requires the basics to get your loved one from point A to point B.

Green burial can be highly cost effective; it's all about simplicity. For instance, you can lower costs by choosing to be buried in a shroud made of a cloth you already own or in a no-frills pine coffin. If you make the coffin yourself, your only cost is the materials. Even a manufactured, biodegradable casket or shroud usually costs less than a conventional casket, which is often made of fabricated steel or lacquered hardwoods. If you forgo embalming, that cost is gone (both conventional and green embalming cost about the same, and both require a professional). Green burials also don't require concrete vaults or liners, which is another cost eliminated.

Headstones are another expense that is highly variable. The grandest headstones can run thousands of dollars, but if you choose a natural marker, or no marker at all, then you pay nothing. Some cemeteries use a GPS system to mark and locate graves, while other cemeteries charge a small fee to place a boulder.

On the other hand, I have known a few instances where a green burial plot was more expensive than a burial space in a standard cemetery. The family chose to bury their loved one in a pricey conservation burial ground, where the cemetery charged a steep fee for the perpetual care of the land. In addition, more specific ongoing maintenance is required for unlined graves, since there isn't a grave liner or box holding up the soil from naturally settling.

Let's take a look at how these costs break down on average:

Modern Burial	Green Burial
Basic services of funeral home: $500–$2000 (Includes arrangement conference, staff, overhead, paperwork assistance, and funeral director guidance.)	Basic services of funeral home: $500–$2,000 DIY funeral: $0
Transportation of remains to funeral home: $250–$650	Transportation of remains to funeral home: $250–$650 Home funeral: $0
Chemical embalming: $250–$500	Green embalming: $250–$500 No embalming: $0
Dressing: $150–$300	Dressing: $0–$300
Casket: $500–$20,000	Casket or shroud: $0–$3,000
Funeral ceremony with viewing: $2,000–$5,000	Funeral ceremony with viewing (no embalming and minimal preparation): $500–$2,000 Home funeral: $0 (or nominal)
Headstone: $500–$5,000	Headstone: $500–$5,000 No grave marker: $0
Grave space: $1,000–$8,000	Grave space: $1,000–$8,000 Backyard grave: $0
Grave liner: $500–$1,500	No grave liner: $0
Opening and closing the grave: $1,000 (Includes digging the grave, preparations for graveside service, refilling the grave, and restoring sod.)	Backyard grave opening and closing: $50–$500 (May involve purchasing supplies, backhoe rental, and so on.)
Hearse to cemetery: $300–$500	Hearse to cemetery: $300–$500 Home funeral with personal transportation or backyard burial: $0

As you can see, green burials and home funerals bypass many of the standard expenses of modern funerals, such as embalming, limousines, vaults, headstone carving, chapel services, and so on. Of course, prices vary widely, and some aspects of a green burial are potentially more expensive in some circumstances. Still, the upshot is that green burials usually save money and save the environment at the same time!

TIP: If you are using a funeral home, always request a recent copy of their general price list (also called a GPL), which is an itemized list of all the goods and services they offer. The "Funeral Rule" of the Federal Trade Commission requires all funeral homes to provide this to anyone making an at-need funeral arrangement. A green burial package should not exceed the cost of an immediate burial package, as essentially you are purchasing a simple burial.

Funeral Wish List

We plan for all major milestones in life, such as a child's birthday and a wedding ceremony. Why wouldn't we plan for our death? As you read this book and consider all the options (as well as any legal issues; see chapter 4), write down your wishes in a list to be eventually shared. This can be a working document that changes over time, but don't keep this information in your head. That won't do your loved ones any good once you're gone.

Here is a list of seven important aspects to consider,

perhaps in consultation with the people you want to carry out your wishes:

1. Who have you appointed to handle your final disposition arrangements? Who is your alternative person, in case the first appointed person is physically or emotionally unable to carry out your wishes?
2. Have you decided to use a traditional funeral home, or someone else, such as a home funeral guide (see page 71)? Or will your funeral be DIY? Does the funeral home or person in charge have your arrangements on file? Have you paid any pre-need costs?
3. What would you like your funeral and burial to look like? Do you want to specify the type of ceremony, or any part of it, such as specific songs, readings, activities, food, or even guests?
4. Is it important to you to have your loved ones view your body? Do you want to specify how a viewing of your body will be handled, and what you will wear?
5. What type of container would you like to be buried in? See chapter 7 for a list of green options, which include a cardboard or wooden casket, a willow or woven coffin, a favorite sleeping bag or comforter, or an organically made outfit or simple shroud.
6. Where would you like to be buried? If a specific cemetery is important, name it, or name the type of place and location, such as conservation grounds or at sea. Consider any specifics about the location that matter to you, such as physical placement on the land. Do you crave to be near a tree? Or the end of a row?

7. What would you like planted or placed on top of your grave? Do you want a specific plant or a standard grave marker? If using a marker, what will it be made out of, and how will it read?

> TIP: To make sure your final wishes are considered legal, I always suggest writing them down and having a notary public stamp and record the document. Notaries are usually on staff at local banks. You can also google for a mobile notary to come to your home if you prefer.

Chapter 4

LEGALITIES TO CONSIDER

This book is not meant to act as a legal guide. In the Resources (page 159), I provide the names of several organizations whose websites contain very helpful and up-to-date legal information. This chapter provides an overview of the main legal issues you need to explore; decide for yourself which pertain to your situation. If you remain uncertain or need more help, consider contacting an attorney.

First and foremost, green burials are legal in every state. But the way burials must be handled can vary. Always double-check with your county to make sure what you are planning to undertake is fully legal where you live.

Do I Need a Funeral Director?

In America, home funerals are legal everywhere. However, as of 2017, nine states require you to appoint a funeral home (and funeral director) for guidance and services. These states are Connecticut, Illinois, Indiana, Iowa, Louisiana, Michigan, Nebraska, New Jersey, and New York.

Here is what these states require, as described by the National Home Funeral Alliance:

> **Connecticut:** Requires a funeral director's signature on the death certificate and bars anyone but a funeral director or embalmer from removing a body or transporting it.
>
> **Illinois:** Defines "funeral director or person acting as such" to include only funeral directors and their employees, according to the Illinois Administrative Code.
>
> **Indiana:** Burial permits can only be given to funeral directors, though other statutes clearly refer broadly to the person in charge of the disposition, e.g., the next of kin.
>
> **Iowa:** Recently changed its law to disallow local registrars from being able to supply burial transit permits, thus forcing families to hire funeral directors or engage medical examiners to file for them.
>
> **Louisiana:** Mandates funeral director involvement in obtaining all necessary permits and funeral director presence at the final disposition of the body. In plain terms, the state literally requires families to hire an undertaker to supervise them.
>
> **Michigan:** Requires that death certificates be "certified" by a funeral director. Additionally, the wills and probate section of the law requires all body dispositions to be conducted by a licensed funeral director.
>
> **Nebraska:** Requires a funeral director to supervise all dispositions and gives funeral directors the right

and authority to issue "transit permits" to move the body out of state.

New Jersey: Requires a funeral director's signature on the death certificate and mandates funeral director presence at the final disposition of the body.

New York: Has requirements similar to Louisiana's.

Of course, every state has specific rules concerning disposition arrangements, and these rules differ, so you need to investigate, understand, and follow the rules where you live. However, all states allow for families to take the lead if they want to handle funeral and burial preparations themselves.

TIP: If the death occurred in a different state than the one where you plan to bury the person, learn the rules and legalities for both states. My funeral home is in Oregon, but I'm close to the border of Washington, where the rules are different.

Appointing Someone to Handle Arrangements

If you hire a licensed funeral director, then that professional will handle and be responsible for following all legal requirements. If you don't work with a funeral director, then it's important to appoint someone to function in this role (or to take on this role yourself for someone else). This person should investigate and understand all the legal issues and assist your family in following them. This is not only to ensure that everyone acts within the scope of the law at all times, but also to ensure the validity of your choices for handling the deceased.

According to USLegal.com, "State legislatures have adopted many statutes that regulate the disposal of dead bodies. Although the right to a decent burial has long been recognized as common law, no universal rule exists as to whom the right of burial is granted." In essence, this means that each state has the right to control disposition, and some states require a licensed funeral director or licensed funeral services practitioner to supervise all aspects of disposition. In other states, only a licensed funeral director may sign and file the death certificate and obtain the burial transit permit, and the family can do everything else.

Consider carefully which person you want to perform the critical role of ensuring that all specific funeral requests are carried out, that all the proper forms are signed, and that the burial proceeds legally. Often, people choose the legal next of kin, which is the simplest way to proceed, but sometimes this isn't the best person for this duty. The next of kin might become emotionally overwhelmed after the death of a loved one. In addition, make sure that the person in charge isn't already in conflict with other family members.

I remember a woman who came into my funeral home and confessed that while she wanted her sister to handle everything when it came to her own funeral, she felt her brother was more appropriate to handle any necessary paperwork. The woman opted to appoint her brother to handle arrangements and her sister to prepare her body for the viewing and to run the burial ceremony. You might want to consider a similar division of duties, one that fits everyone's strengths.

The Order of Next of Kin

Typically, you will designate a close relative, next of kin, or power of attorney for health care who will be the person to make final disposition decisions. Some states also recognize your authority to name your own funeral arrangements in a will or living trust. If no one is specified, then this duty automatically falls to the next of kin.

To qualify as next of kin, a person must be over eighteen years old and deemed mentally sound. Here is a partial list that reflects the order in most states:

- Spouse (or registered domestic partner)
- Children (normally starting with eldest legal offspring)
- Parents
- Siblings
- Grandchildren
- Grandparents
- Nieces and nephews
- Aunts and uncles
- Great-grandchildren
- Great-grandparents
- Great-nieces and -nephews
- First cousins
- Great-aunts and -uncles
- Great-great-grandchildren, and so on

Basically, the order of next of kin continues until all potential relatives, no matter how distant, are exhausted, and only then would a friend be considered next of kin. It doesn't matter how close or long-term your relationship is — whether the person is your live-in girlfriend, boyfriend, significant other, or life partner. In the eyes of the law, unrelated, unmarried people are designated as "friends" and fall to the end of the list. So, again, if you want someone who is not related to you to be your legal next of kin, please take the time now to draw up and legally execute the correct document.

However, one thing to keep in mind is that documents like a living trust are not accessible until after death. If the person designated to handle funeral arrangements is not already aware of your choices, that person may not learn of your wishes in time to carry them out. That is why it is so important to discuss your choice for natural burial with your family before your death.

For instance, this happened with a woman named Trish, who called me at my funeral home quite upset after she learned she was chosen by her best friend to be the person to carry out her funeral wishes. But Trish hadn't been told beforehand, and she only learned of it three weeks after the friend's cremation. The will had been locked in a safety deposit box, which the next of kin couldn't access until a funeral home was chosen, arrangements were made, and a certified copy of the death certificate was received and brought to the bank that held the will. Not only that, but the deceased had wanted a green burial. Trish was distraught that she hadn't been able to provide her best friend with what she wanted, even though Trish wasn't to blame. The whole thing could have been avoided with better planning by her well-meaning friend.

Finally, if you feel it will be difficult or even impossible for a friend or family member to honor all your wishes for your burial, you can prepay a funeral home for an itemized contract of goods and services. This way, before your death, you've already outlined and paid for what you want to be done.

> TIP: If you trust your survivors to carry out your wishes and you're not concerned with making them ironclad, you may use whatever method you like to make your preferences clear. Contracts and lawyers aren't necessary if verbal agreements will do.

Home Burial Packets

If you are planning a loved one's funeral and burial without hiring help, make sure to get something called a home burial packet or home funeral packet, which contains important forms (saving you the time and trouble of gathering them) and information on the rules for your state, which sometimes vary. Most mortuary boards, funeral bureaus, and cemetery licensing departments make these packets available upon request to the general public. In some states, packets can be downloaded online. A home burial packet should be requested by anyone who has been appointed to handle funeral arrangements or by families who are holding home funerals without the assistance of a funeral home, which typically charges to take care of filing the death certificate.

If a person is in hospice, or has been told that death is imminent, the person acting as a funeral service practitioner should call for a packet. Do not wait until the death has occurred.

As an example, the Oregon home funeral packet contains the following:

- An Oregon death certificate and the instructions for completing the death certificate, which includes time-sensitive information.
- An identification tag, which must be attached to the receptacle containing human remains. The number on the identifying metal disc is placed on the upper left-hand corner of the death certificate.
- Facts about funeral and cemetery arrangements (which are provided by all states' funeral boards or bureaus).
- A fact sheet on the burial of human remains on private property.

Above all, these packets serve to give practical information on how to learn about, plan for, and carry out a green burial. Reviewing this information sooner rather than later can help you decide whether (and in what ways) you might want to work with a funeral home.

Filing for a Certificate of Death

In the United States, it is legal for families to prepare and convey a dead body for disposition. However, if you choose to take full possession of your loved one's body, you must take care of the legal paperwork that must accompany the body. Research this ahead of time, since the process can vary depending on the state where the death occurred. Ultimately, you will need a properly completed certificate of death, which is signed by the attending physician, medical examiner, or coroner (depending on the state).

The certificate of death then needs to be filed with the registrar for the county where the death took place. This might be the town clerk if you are burying in a rural area or the city registrar in cities. Once this is done, the municipal registrar will issue you a permit for disposition. Some states allow a temporary permit before the death certificate is registered. This document goes by different names, but it is the legal permit you need to transport a body and accompany it to its final place of disposition, whether cremation, burial in a cemetery, or anatomical donation.

Chapter 5

IT TAKES A VILLAGE

Getting Help and Hiring Professionals

W hen someone is transitioning out of this world, many providers are needed. You simply can't do it alone. Figuratively and literally, funerals take many hands. Green burial is all about building and leaning on community.

Corpse wrapped in green and pink blankets on pine boughs in Native American ceremony (Photo credit: Gail Rubin, CT, agoodgoodbye.com)

It takes a village to raise a child. It also takes a village to bury the dead.

Everyone has strengths and weaknesses, so consider the best ways for others to help. When someone is dying, certain individuals may be better at pain management and emotional comfort, someone else may help with religious and spiritual needs, and someone else might organize visitations. You will need all avenues of support with the funeral as well. Surround yourself with community, one with a centered response that recognizes death as a natural, accepted, and honored part of life.

Consider how your existing community can be helpful: Can you put together a team from your personal and social connections to oversee and take on the practical steps needed for a successful home funeral and green burial? Without hiring a professional, can you assemble a tribe of loving souls who have both the understanding and the skills to accomplish the burial that you, or the deceased, want? Will you be comfortable handling the body (see chapter 8)? If not, a range of professional help is available.

TIP: No matter what type of funeral you have, make sure to appoint a photographer, even if it's just a friend using the built-in camera on their cell phone. Designate someone to regularly snap photos who will feel at ease documenting the journey, even if the moments are very personal and photography seems intrusive.

As we all maneuver along our spiritual path, we ultimately discover that death truly links us to life and community. Even in death, people want to be remembered for how they brought people together and gave back to the world.

Hiring a Funeral Home

Even if you're planning both a home funeral and a green burial, a funeral home can sometimes provide helpful or necessary assistance. Many funeral homes are advocates of natural burial, even though funeral directors go to school to learn how to preserve a body, not conserve the environment.

Hiring a funeral home to file the death certificate can be very helpful. They do this daily, and the office staff know how to maneuver through all the various legal and bureaucratic channels to locate a doctor, fill out the form properly, get it signed, and then file it with the right agency. Funeral homes can file the certificate electronically if their state uses this method. An electronic death certificate speeds up the signing and certifying process, since there's no need to courier documents around town.

Funeral homes can assist with lots of practical details: They have vehicles built for transporting bodies, a facility for services, and products like burial containers suitable for your needs. You can hire a funeral home to help with only one or two tasks, or funeral homes can facilitate the entire service in many shades of green.

That said, not all funeral homes are equally open to green burial. You want to find a funeral home that supports or adheres to the practices of natural burial and that will be willing to help in whatever ways you ask.

To begin the search process, visit the Green Burial Council website (see Resources). Their provider page lists parlors nationwide that follow up-to-date standards and have packages for green burial services. Identify a few providers who are conveniently located to the deceased, and make some calls. Even if your local funeral home is not on this list, call them as well and get a feel for their willingness to help.

Here is a series of questions to ask funeral directors. Modify these depending on your needs:

> Have they helped other families with green funeral
> and burial services?
> Do they have a package for these services on their
> general price list (or GPL)?
> Do they offer eco-embalming, or will they allow a
> visitation without embalming?
> Will they allow you to transport your own deceased
> loved one?
> Will they work with you to carry out your vision of a
> home funeral or green burial?

Consider not just the funeral home's specific answers but their attitude. Do they take the time to listen to your needs and agree to help where they can? Does personalization work with how they run their business, or do you hear the words, "That isn't how we do things"? If you meet lots of confrontation, objections, or silence, move on and keep looking. Some families are fortunate enough to have the means and wherewithal to fully oversee and care for their dead. If you are not in that situation, please be gentle with yourself. You have not failed your loved one. Life sometimes throws a few curves in the plan, but funeral homes have capabilities and can be used for as little or as much support as you need to get through your tough time.

Greenwashing

As demand for green services and products grows, so does "greenwashing," which is the term for a company or organization that spends more time and money claiming to be "green" than actually implementing business practices that minimize environmental impact. The Green Burial Council defines greenwashing as "the disingenuous act of making a product, service, or facility appear to be providing some environmental benefit, when in fact it does not." The Green Burial Council and other regulating bodies are working to develop standards to prevent greenwashing.

So, as you evaluate funeral homes, be on the lookout for greenwashing. Don't take every marketing or advertising claim at face value. Since consumers are increasingly seeking out and willing to pay more for clearly green products, it's not surprising that instances of greenwashing are on the rise. For help and advice, consult the Green Burial Council, whose mission includes ensuring accountability among providers of all things green burial.

Death Care Consultants

There are other professionals besides funeral homes you can hire to help. In Oregon, we have what are called "death care consultants," though these professionals have different titles in other states. These are people who can consult on matters related to funeral or final disposition arrangements. The difference between them and a funeral home (or "funeral service provider") is that a death care consultant cannot provide any direct physical assistance with, or supervision of, handling the body, but they are a great resource to hire for individuals who want to act as their own funeral service provider. Consultants do not serve the same apprenticeship or take the same exam as a funeral director, even though consultants can handle a lot of the same facets of funerals and burials.

End-of-Life Doulas

Just like midwives who help with birth, there are now "midwives" who help with death. As medicine has advanced, sometimes we have let technology overwhelm the mortal dimension. Sometimes we need an experienced person who can be fully present with someone as they die, and then be fully present with the family to help with post-death needs. "Like birth, death is one of life's most important transitions for a human," notes Richard Gunderman in *The Atlantic*.

Sometimes referred to as a death doula or death midwife, an end-of-life doula can provide emotional, psychological, and spiritual support to the patient, family, and community during all stages of dying, death, grieving, and burial. They are not licensed funeral directors or certified or registered nurses, but they help the person who is dying, and they help the family create healing rituals after death. Cassandra Yonder calls death midwifery "a grassroots response to the cultural alienation we are feeling from dying, death, post-death care, and grief."

To be clear, end-of-life doulas are not hired to take over various tasks for the family, such as filling out and filing the death-related paperwork or transporting the deceased to the place of burial. Think of this person as an end-of-life guide who helps the family and the dying person through the final period of living up until the moment of death.

Home Funeral Guides

Another important role in the death-care continuum is the home funeral guide. This person empowers the decedent's family and friends to care for their own dead and guides them through the steps of after-death care. This trained individual can oversee the body's preparations, although the physical work is done by the family. A home funeral guide serves as a coach — as someone who lovingly empowers a family to conduct the tasks of taking care of their own dead.

End-of-life doulas and home funeral guides are not the same. According to Lee Webster, founding member of the National End-of-Life Doula Alliance and former president of the National Home Funeral Alliance, "There is a distinct legal difference and set of regulations that oversee pre- and post-death care....Can someone be both? Certainly, but not necessarily. Are they interchangeable? No."

Nancy Ward, who runs Sacred Endings in Scappoose, Oregon, says about home funeral guiding, "It's a lost art. We're bringing back a tradition where we empower the family to do a sacred duty."

Chapter 6

A PLACE TO REST

Green Cemeteries and Backyard Burials

The basic tenets of environmentally friendly living are now being posed for environmentally friendly dying. Green burial is all about sustainability and developing funeral practices that support and heal nature rather than disrupt and harm it. One key to the natural-burial movement is green or natural cemeteries, much like the town churchyard and farmer's field where bodies were once buried in a shroud or biodegradable box. Today, modern cemeteries have almost completely replaced these practices, but the good news is that traditional cemeteries are on the decline. They are losing business to cremation, and with green burials on the rise, green cemeteries are appearing to accommodate them.

However, for many, there's something appealing about the return to family cemetery plots on family land. Of course, this practice enjoys a very, very long tradition in America. It's what families did for generations — burying loved ones on the family property. So, this chapter first looks at green cemeteries, and then it describes what you need to know to conduct your own backyard burial, including how to properly dig a grave. Finally, it briefly explores a third green burial option: burial at sea.

Green Burial Grounds and Cemeteries

A green cemetery doesn't try to control nature with pesticides, pristine lawns, nonbiodegradable caskets, and concrete burial vaults. Green burial grounds allow the physical world to bloom and blossom; they encourage the indigenous shrubs, wildflowers, woodlands, and grasslands that support the area's birds and other wildlife.

Of course, you may or may not be able to find a genuinely green cemetery where you live. However, some traditional cemeteries allow certain green practices, so always ask. For instance, according to the National Funeral Directors Association, "The use of outer burial containers or vaults is not required by federal or state law, but is required by many cemeteries. In many rural areas, vaults or grave liners are usually not required." The reason traditional cemeteries usually require a vault is to keep their graveyards from developing a wavy-gravy look. Once biodegradable caskets decompose, the earth will settle, leaving depressions.

The Three Categories of Green Burial Grounds

The Green Burial Council distinguishes three types of green burial grounds: hybrid, natural, and conservation. Here is their official definition of each:

Hybrid Burial Grounds are conventional cemeteries offering the option for burial without the need for a vault (partial, inverted, or otherwise), a vault lid, concrete box, slab, or partitioned liner. Hybrid Burial Grounds shall not require the embalming of decedents and must allow for any kind of eco-friendly burial containers, including shrouds.

Natural Burial Grounds require the adoption of practices/protocols that are energy-conserving, minimize waste, and do not require the use of toxic chemicals. A Natural Burial Ground achieves GBC certification by prohibiting the use of vaults (partial, inverted, or otherwise), vault lids, concrete boxes, slabs, or partitioned liners, and by prohibiting the burial of decedents embalmed with toxic chemicals, as well as by banning burial containers not made from natural/plant-derived materials. It must have in place a program of Integrated Pest Management (IPM) and be designed, operated, and maintained to produce a naturalistic appearance, based on use of plants and materials native to the region, and patterns of landscape derived from and compatible with regional ecosystems.

Conservation Burial Grounds, in addition to meeting all the requirements for a Natural Burial Ground, must further legitimate land conservation. It must protect in perpetuity an area of land specifically and exclusively designated for conservation. A Conservation Burial Ground must involve an established conservation organization that holds a conservation easement or has in place a deed restriction guaranteeing long-term stewardship.

If there is not a natural or conservation burial ground close to you, a hybrid burial ground may be easier to find. These are standard cemeteries that typically have an area set aside that does not require a casket or grave liner. Cemeteries all over the country are considering and opening sections for natural burial spaces, so never hesitate to pick up the phone and ask your local cemetery directly.

As you research possible cemeteries, you will find some graveyards are set in very contemporary, natural environs. Williamsburg Cemetery in Kitchener, Ontario, boasts beautiful wetlands, encourages bird-watching, and has natural walking trails and ponds; this cemetery has fully integrated their burial areas in a natural-looking garden. But despite this serene and reflective exterior, all gravesites require liners, and therefore this cannot be considered a hybrid, natural, or conservation cemetery.

For a list of green burial grounds in the United States and Canada, see page 163.

What If You Already Own Cemetery Lots?

As I've said, most local cemeteries require the use of a burial vault to maintain flat ground in their memorial park. However, ask if the cemetery will allow for the burial vault to be placed upside down, over the top of the casket. This helps ensure two things: The casket can be as close to the ground as possible, so the deceased will eventually rejoin with the earth, and yet this still provides a suitable surface for maintaining level ground.

Obviously, if you are paying for a grave space at a green burial cemetery or hybrid cemetery, they have you covered. You'll be able to have a green burial, and you won't need to worry about the logistics, as you do with a backyard burial. Still, if using your own John Deere and making your own hole in the ground is important to you, you need to find a different location than a traditional cemetery.

Backyard Burials

A backyard burial encompasses burying a person on residential property, or land that is privately owned. This precludes any land that has been endorsed as an actual cemetery. Most bodies are buried in established cemeteries, but burial on private property may be possible. Laws vary not only state

Backyard burial in very sandy soil (Photo credit: Elizabeth Fournier)

to state but county to county; it's most accepted and typical in rural settings.

If you are considering a backyard burial, think carefully about what it may mean for the property itself and the person who owns it (which may be yourself). All other issues aside, burying someone on private land impacts the future sale of that property. In addition, however remote the concern may be, you should consider how you'd feel, and what you would do, if your deceased loved one resided on property that you no longer owned.

For instance, depending on the type of property, the land could become fundamentally unmarketable to succeeding buyers if the interred body isn't relocated, and even then, a stigma might remain that makes selling the tract difficult. Not only that, exhuming and transferring a body is expensive. However, even if this isn't done and the property is sold, family members and others won't necessarily have access to the property to visit the gravesite anymore. Perhaps most unsettling of all, what if the land is sold and developed for a different use, one that rattles the bones in their resting place?

In light of these issues, reflect on all the possible outcomes before committing to creating a private burial ground on residentially zoned property. Further, don't make this decision without legal guidance and consultation, and begin the planning process well in advance. It can involve a lot of paperwork.

But do not let these cautions discourage you if this is your dream or the final wishes of someone you love. I am truly finding that people are increasingly embracing the mindset of ashes to ashes and dust to dust, and many families I have served would not have done it any other way.

Legal Considerations with Residential Burials

Regarding the future sale of the property, it is the responsibility of the property owner to disclose if human remains are buried anywhere on the land. The owner must agree to maintain and provide records of the disposition on the property, and agree to disclose the disposition of human remains upon sale of the property.

As for the legality of the burial itself, the property will be governed by local laws, so consult with your local health authority prior to planning the burial. Personally, I run every address by my county's zoning and planning department just to make sure. For this guidebook, I hesitate to generalize, as the rules vary by county and town. In essence, private property burial is often allowed, but each area has slightly different requirements.

One thing you must do, no matter whose name is on the property's deed, is to get the written consent of any mortgage or lien holders. As well, you must meet all state requirements for the completion of the death certificate and acquire all transport permits or other required documentation.

Home burials in Oregon must meet certain environmental standards. For instance, land in which surface water or ground drainage enters other water sources — like a pond, stream, well, tributary, and so on — cannot be used for burial purposes without written approval from the Oregon Department of Environmental Protection. I've read other regulations that stipulate that private burial sites "should be

150 feet from a water supply, 100 feet from a drilled well, and 25 feet from a power line....It's also a good idea to bury at least 20 feet from the setback on your property." Finally, even when you can create a family burial ground on your own land, you cannot charge money for burial rites. Most people wouldn't, but this is just an example of the many issues and concerns you should investigate before moving forward.

> TIP: Mother Nature Network offers this excellent advice: "If you bury a body on private land, you should draw a map of the property showing the burial ground and file it with the property deed so the location will be clear to others in the future."

How to Dig a Grave

Traditionally, back in the day, the church sexton was the person in charge of digging and preparing the gravesite at a cemetery. This was part of the sexton's overall duties to maintain the church grounds and buildings. Today, cemeteries usually have or hire a crew to help with these responsibilities. If you are undertaking your own backyard burial, this section will guide you in doing this yourself.

The first thing to consider is where to place the grave. You will want an area clear of obvious boulders and tree roots, and the type of soil can make a big difference in digging. According to the website Funeral Helper, "Heavy clay soils will require much greater effort to excavate than finer, richer soils. If very sandy soil is present, then burials are not

Opening of burial trench in grass field on private land (Photo credit: Elizabeth Fournier)

recommended, as the risk of it collapsing and therefore the risk of injury is high."

Then, is it really true you must bury a body "six feet under"? No. In fact, graves only need to be three or four feet deep. According to *Mental Floss* magazine, the phrase "six feet under" came from a 1665 flu epidemic in England, which wiped out a lot of citizens. London's mayor "laid down the law about how to deal with all of the future dead bodies to avoid further infections." Today, cemeteries only dig graves that are six or seven feet deep when they plan to place another body on top of it in the future. In the funeral industry, we call this a double grave, double depth, double stacked, or even bunk beds.

TALES FROM THE GRAVE

If you're having a backyard burial, be thankful it's no longer the Middle Ages in Western Europe. Since people were afraid that a dead person's spirit might return to haunt the living and cause trouble, morticians decapitated cadavers before burial. According to a story in the *Houston Chronicle*, "For those who had committed suicide, more drastic measures were taken; a mortician would thrust a stake through the deceased's heart at midnight."

Digging the Grave and Preparing for Burial

Digging a grave is hard work. Don't let images you've seen on movies or television fool you. It takes a lot of time and energy to move many pounds of dirt. On average, with two or more people digging with shovels, it will take about three hours to dig a four-foot-deep grave. Obviously, measure the coffin or container to be buried very carefully to determine the size of the hole. The last thing you want is a grave that's too short or too narrow, nor do you want to dig more than you need to. On average, graves are about thirty-six inches wide by eighty-four inches long to accommodate grave liners or standard-size caskets, but with backyard burials you have the flexibility to create a custom-sized grave as long as the chosen burial container will lower and rest comfortably inside the space.

As for digging tools, you have two basic choices: backhoe or shovel. Two different methods, and two completely different experiences and time frames. If you're digging by hand, use a long-handled, steel shovel. The long handle is preferable to minimize back pain or strain from standing, bending, and shoveling for long periods of time. A square-shaped model works very well for moving dirt and small rocks.

As for a backhoe, I recommend a small rubber-tracked excavator, with a backfill blade on the front, because of their small size and agility. Once positioned, these small earth-movers can dig 360 degrees and usually handle a bigger bucket than a compact tractor-mounted backhoe. I believe some even have special buckets just for digging graves to give you that square-cornered, flat bottom. If you're digging a deeper grave, you might want an extended hoe for extra reach and depth. That said, green burials often discourage using heavy machinery for digging graves in order to preserve the natural setting as much as possible.

TIP: According to professional gravediggers, shovel slowly and steadily and "begin your dirt pile far from the hole, so there is room nearby to put the last shovelfuls when fatigue sets in and you're deep in your first grave." In addition, bring a small ladder, so that it's easy to get out of the grave at the end of a tiring day!

Here are some step-by-step instructions for digging a grave and preparing the gravesite for a ceremony. These are adapted from advice given by Britain's Jonny Yaxley, who was named England's Gravedigger of the Year in 2014.

- Outline the dimensions to be dug with sand, string, or preferably some organic material. (Yaxley uses spray paint.)
- Cut along the outline with a spade, and then remove strips of turf as carefully as possible, arranging them like jigsaw pieces on plywood sheets laid nearby. (Yaxley removes the turf with an excavator claw.)
- Dig the grave and level the bottom. Stand on the rim and smooth the sidewalls with a heavy spade.
- For appearance, line the bottom of the grave with sawdust, twigs, or leaves.
- Position wood board planks along the edge of the hole to ensure firm footing for the pallbearers.
- If you wish, use rolls of artificial turf to cover any dirt or areas around the grave that might be unsightly to the mourners.
- On the carpet in front of the hole, lay two wooden beams on which the coffin or shroud will rest. On the beams, lay out whatever webbing, ropes, or straps you will use to lower the deceased into the ground.

TALES FROM THE GRAVE

In 2016, the second annual Grave Digging Competition saw ten, two-person teams from Slovakia, Poland, and Hungary compete to see who would win the crown as the fastest gravediggers in Europe. The winning team, from Slovakia, dug their grave in less than an hour.

Lowering the Body and Closing the Grave

Since the burial is not happening at a cemetery, a proper lowering device will not be on hand. This means ropes or straps are the only way to make sure the coffin, basket, or other biodegradable container is lowered smoothly and completely. It works best if six to eight physically capable people help with the lowering, and if each person holds their own strap or rope. If you're concerned about weight, I recommend using more handles and more attendants. Better too many than too few, and remember: Slow and steady!

If the deceased is being buried in a shroud or nonrigid container, realize that bodies don't distribute their weight evenly. Lowering will go smoother if the body is placed on a solid wood board. Sometimes shrouds have a two-by-four sewn inside as well. You will want to deal with these logistics before your arrival at the deceased's new resting place.

Opened grave ready to receive loved one for burial at Gibson Cemetery, Estacada, OR (Photo credit: Elizabeth Fournier)

After the body has been lowered into the grave and the service has been completed, it will be time to close the grave. Often, replacing the dirt is incorporated into the funeral ritual itself. This might be merely ceremonial, with people tossing handfuls of dirt over the body, or it could be more robust, with family and friends taking turns returning whole shovelfuls of earth.

Completed burial at the Meadow Natural Burial Grounds at Greenacres Memorial Park, Ferndale, WA (Photo credit: Elizabeth Fournier)

When this is done and the mourners have gone, or once everyone is ready for the next step of the process, return to complete backfilling and closing the grave. Using either shovels or machinery, return all the previously removed dirt. If you set aside portions of turf, restore these. Either way, it's best to leave the grave somewhat rounded on top, since some settling will occur as the container and body decompose over time. Later, to maintain the ethos of natural burial, plant only native species of vegetation and flowers over the grave.

For examples of green burials, please see chapter 9.

Burial at Sea

Burial at sea is a disposition method that releases a deceased body into the ocean, so that it sinks and decomposes naturally. A burial at sea can be considered a green burial if, as with any green burial, it does not involve traditional embalming or containers made of steel, concrete, or other nonbiodegradable materials.

Arranging a burial at sea is possible for anyone, no matter how far from the water you live. However, it requires a boat, and if you don't have one, you'll need to contract one. Also, a burial at sea (as well as spreading cremated ashes at sea) must follow a different set of rules than for burials on land.

The Environmental Protection Agency (EPA) oversees US laws and regulations for burials at sea. The general permit is published in the federal regulations (available online; see endnotes), and the rules mandate that the site of the water interment be three nautical miles from land and at a depth of at least six hundred feet. Furthermore, the rule requires that "all necessary measures shall be taken to ensure that the remains sink to the bottom rapidly and permanently."

New England Burials at Sea is a Massachusetts company

that can be hired for this service, and they also provide help and information for families interested in this option. I had a lovely email exchange with the owner, Captain Brad White, who said voyages take about forty-five minutes to reach the desired location, approximately three miles off the coast at an ocean depth of six hundred feet.

Performing a green burial at sea is possible without the help of a contracted service. If you wish to do so, consult the EPA's "Burial at Sea" website, and keep these two important steps in mind:

- The EPA must be notified within thirty days of a full-body burial at sea with the following details: date, time, place, name of the deceased, and person responsible for burying the body at sea.
- Care needs to be taken to ensure that the body sinks to the ocean floor. Either weigh down a biodegradable shroud, or drill a natural wood coffin with enough holes that it will take on water (the EPA website has instructions).

TALES FROM THE GRAVE

Osama bin Laden is buried at sea. His body was transported by the USS *Carl Vinson* aircraft carrier and let loose into the Arabian Sea. According to writer David Gilson, "You could say Osama bin Laden had received the ultimate green burial, courtesy of the United States Navy."

Chapter 7

GREEN BURIAL CONTAINERS

Handmade Caskets and Shrouds

The best caskets are joyful epitaphs in wood.

— Steve Maxwell

To have a truly green burial, the body should be buried in clothing and a container made of 100-percent natural, biodegradable materials. This allows everything that is buried to decompose and return to the soil. Most people prefer to be buried in a casket or coffin, and using a natural one made of untreated wood like pine is an ideal, green choice. These can be handmade to order, or you can make your own (see page 92). However, new types of burial containers are being developed all the time, ones that use eco-friendly, organic materials like wicker, bamboo, willow, hemp, banana leaves, and sea grass.

People can also forgo a box and be buried in a cloth shroud. With green burial, the concern isn't only what we put into the ground, but the amount of resources we use to bury ourselves. After all, we came into this world possessing only a body. How much does our body really need when we leave it?

Handmade Natural Coffins

The tenets of natural burial resonate with those who want to honor and support our planet. This includes many talented woodworkers who are joining the green burial movement by building caskets in harmony with nature. These craftspeople see themselves as responsible stewards of Earth's resources, which is another way to understand what it means to rest in peace.

A casket doesn't just hold and display the body and supply a receptacle for burial. It provides your loved one with an environmentally sound choice at the end of life. This can be part of their legacy for the next generation. Usually made of pine, poplar, oak, or maple, these natural caskets look similar to a traditional casket, but they are more environmentally friendly. If untreated wood isn't appealing, biodegradable finishes can be used.

Typically, any local woodworker should be able to make a custom wood casket. They are simple to construct. Obviously, prices vary depending on the cost of materials and the construction itself, but expect to spend at least $400.

You might request that, if they don't already, the woodworker use local trees that have already fallen and repurpose them into custom pieces. My casket maker, Richard, builds solidly rustic caskets out of western red cedar that falls on his property. His serene haven of a shop sits in the midst of these soaring trees overlooking the Clackamas River Basin. He started building natural caskets when he received a request from a fellow veteran. Richard spends three to four days carefully crafting each piece by hand, and he finds this adds a little peace for grieving families.

TALES FROM THE GRAVE

In Ghana, "fantasy coffins" are constructed to represent the deceased's job or life passions. They are produced from wood and then shaped and painted into everything from soda bottles and rocket ships to zoo animals. I know a woman in Manhattan who has her Empire State Building casket propped up against her apartment living room wall, just waiting for the day she needs it.

Shelves for Life

If you like to plan ahead, consider ordering a bookcase from Shelves for Life. Invented by designer William Warren, these shelving units function like standard shelves while you are alive. When death knocks on the door, the shelves can be taken apart and reassembled as a coffin. Since this product uses a few pieces of small metal hardware, it's not purely eco-friendly. Still, as Mother Nature Network observed, "Producing a new coffin is extremely energy- and resource-intensive and by being buried in a piece of repurposed furniture you completely avoid the unsustainable getting-buried-in-a-new-coffin thing."

How to Make a Natural Wood Casket

Handmade natural cedar casket made by Oregon artisan Richard Clarke (Photo credit: Richard Clarke)

I asked my casket maker, Richard, for advice on how to make a casket, and here is his quick-and-easy method.

1. Use a shoebox as your scaled-down model for your finished casket. Mark it with measurements for all necessary cuts.
2. Carefully measure the person who will be in the casket. A standard casket is eighty inches long, twenty-eight inches wide, and twenty-three inches high (these are all external measurements), but you may

need more or less wood to complete the job. Also find out what specific objects will be placed inside the casket so you can allow for extra room.

3. Use the wood you have on hand or have experience working with, but reclaimed wood is always a great choice. Avoid plywood, which is usually too thin for this project.

4. If you are making a rectangular casket, you can cut the base and lid at the same time, the sides at the same time, and the top and bottom at the same time. If you create a tapered design, cut the base and lid at the same time, and the top and bottom at the same time. For the sides, cut four separate pieces: two shorter pieces for the upper (tapered) side of the casket, and two longer pieces for the lower. Using screws, attach the walls to the base. Hinges can be used to attach the lid to the bottom half of the container. Then, one by one, remove the screws and add a wood dowel and seal the seams and screw holes with nontoxic wood glue.

5. To create handles, use about 24 feet of strong rope or nylon cord, and drill holes along the sides of the casket, through which you will weave the rope. Drill three holes on the lower portion of each long side, and two holes on each end, top and bottom. Weave the rope or cord through these openings, which creates a secured grouping of six handles for attendants to carry the casket. Make sure to tie off the ends of the rope firmly (on the inside), and use nontoxic wood glue to secure the knots, if needed.

6. If you want a soft casket liner, sew this out of bio-degradable silk or cotton (or hire an experienced seamstress to do this), and attach. You can also have your loved one lie on a soft comforter, sheet, non-synthetic pillows, or nothing at all.

Green Burial Shrouds

A burial shroud is simply any piece of fabric used to wrap a body. The Green Burial Council declares that a "shroud is suitable for a green burial if it's made from materials/substances that are nontoxic and readily biodegradable." A shroud-wrapped body can be placed inside a casket or directly into a grave.

Families often tell me their loved one wants to be wrapped in a basic sheet, comforter, or blanket. Great! As long as it is made out of something 100-percent biodegradable (such as cotton, wool, silk, and so on), that makes for an ideal green burial. Previously used fabrics, like wall tapestries and linen tablecloths, also can work well.

If you plan to bury someone in only a shroud, do heed my warning above: Place some sort of board under the body for lowering into the grave. A few ropes make an awkward support for a floppy human bundle.

If you would like to design your own burial shroud, follow the simple instructions below.

How to Make a Green Burial Shroud

A shroud can be simple or elaborate, a single piece of material or a hand-sewn masterpiece. Most families need some sort of shroud fairly quickly after a death has occurred. Therefore, hiring a last-minute shroud maker or seamstress isn't always feasible. These basic instructions will give you an idea of how easy and satisfying making your own shroud can be. (Images were designed by Pashta MaryMoon and adapted for this book.)

1. Find a piece of 100 percent biodegradable fabric, such as natural or organic cotton, wool, linen, silk, bamboo fleece, muslin, cheesecloth, hemp, cashmere, or jute. Cut the material into a square large enough that the body can be placed on it with the head at one corner and the feet at the opposite corner, with twelve to twenty-four inches of extra fabric above the head and below the feet. Work on a clean, flat surface large enough to hold the body and with enough space around it that you and any helpers will be able to move around it as necessary. A table, a bed, or the floor can work well, although the floor can be problematic if the body is heavier. Preferably, the body will be naked, or it may be dressed in natural-fiber (biodegradable) clothing or already wrapped in a sheet. Spread out the fabric on the work surface, and position the body on top of it. (See figure 1.)

2. Fold the extra material below the feet up onto the legs. Next, fold the extra material above the head down toward the chest. Make sure there is a little slack. (See figure 2.)

3. Wrap the extra fabric from one side across the body, and tuck it underneath. Do the same with the extra fabric from the other side, and tuck that piece

completely under the shroud. The body should appear cocoon-like and cozy. (See figure 3.)

4. If you have extra material left over, cut it into strips long enough to tie around the shroud. If not, use rope, cotton ties, or any other natural textile that can be used as straps. Start with the feet: securely tie a strap around the lower calves/ankles, making sure all the material is still tucked in and smooth. Move up to the waist area and slide a strap under the body and tie it firmly in the front. The tie should go over the hands/ wrists to secure the arms into place. Finally, when you feel ready, tightly tuck the flap over the face and tie the strap firmly around the neck. (See figure 4.)

Figure 1.

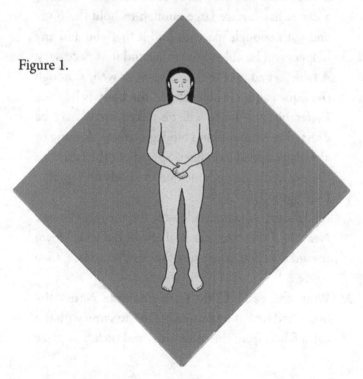

Figure 2.

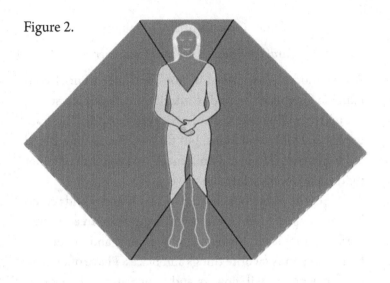

Figure 3.

Figure 4.

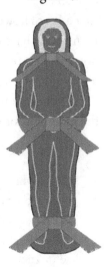

Other Green Burial Containers

Cardboard and Fiberboard Containers

A very modest, low-priced option for a green burial container is fiberboard or cardboard. Both materials are strong enough to hold a body and are rather eco-friendly. These are used mainly for cremations, but they will work for a burial as long as there is a board underneath to keep the container rigid while lowering into the grave.

Since these can look utilitarian, family and friends could be encouraged to decorate them using toxic-free colored markers, nonplastic stickers, family photos, and pictures of their loved one's favorite things and places. I have often seen them covered in wildflowers and boughs from the woods. Families will also line the casket with a soft down comforter or blanket and maybe a pure cotton pillow. If the deceased isn't a fan of flowers, instead of sprinkling the cardboard box with petals, have everyone write farewell messages on sticky notes and place them on the box. I have seen this done, and it was quite lovely!

If you want to construct your own cardboard coffin, see the endnotes for resources.

TIP: If your green burial isn't on private property, be sure to check with your chosen cemetery about the type of container you're planning to use. Cemeteries have the right to decide what they will allow to be buried on their property.

Infinity Burial Suits and Shrouds

The company Coeio produces green burial items that are unlike anything else on the market. For instance, the Infinity Burial Suit and the Infinity Burial Shroud are special clothing infused full of mushroom spores and fungi. The spores speed decomposition, remediate toxins, spur plant growth, and improve soil quality, thus returning your body to the earth and the ongoing cycle of life without harming the ecosystem. Of course, this organic technology must be used on its own, without any sort of casket, vault, or traditional burial container. According to the product's website, the Infinity Burial Suit "cleanses the body and the soil of toxins that would otherwise seep into the environment." However, I'm not sure our bodies contain so much toxic gunk that we leave poisonous carcasses.

Ecopods

Ecopods are a natural burial chest that was designed by English midwife Hazel Selina. The "eco" part of the name refers to its composition — it's made from both recycled newspapers and handmade mulberry paper, and is thus biodegradable. And the "pod" part... well, it looks like a giant seed pod. Ecopods are offered in a range of colors, including red with an Aztec sun design, but as of publication, they were temporarily out of production. The company is currently exploring different production options and hoping to partner with the Natural Burial Company in Eugene, Oregon.

Chapter 8

GREEN EMBALMING AND HANDLING THE BODY

*I*n addition to discussing green embalming, this chapter provides you with the guidance, tools, and loving support for successfully preparing a body for burial.

Of course, lovingly taking care of our deceased loved one is a central goal of green burials and home funerals. But we cannot forget to take care of ourselves as well. When a person dies, someone needs to be in charge of handling the body and, if necessary, preserving it until burial. Ask yourself: Do you have the stamina and emotional capacity to handle the body without the assistance of a funeral home, or would you prefer hiring someone else? Check in with yourself honestly about this decision.

Green Embalming

First, embalming is never required by any state or federal law. Second, embalming is usually only necessary when a body is kept out of refrigeration for a certain length of time, if the body will be shipped on a common carrier airline, and for public visitations and mausoleum entombment. Embalming is a process of substituting bodily fluids with chemicals to slow decay and preserve the body. This procedure is always handled by a licensed embalmer at a funeral facility.

For a few days, refrigeration works just fine to stave off rapid decomposition (see more below), and a body can be viewed that hasn't been embalmed. But some families choose embalming, not only to preserve a body until burial, but because this technique allows color to return to the very pale complexion of a lifeless body. In our American culture, we often feel the need to preserve the body and, as much as possible, to restore a lifelike presence. This can also be done with organic embalming fluid.

Green embalming fluids are made of a variety of non-toxic, all-natural, biodegradable, plant-based extracts. While formulations differ, green embalming is always formaldehyde-free, which protects the embalmer and nature from this toxin. Green embalming extends the time available for transportation and viewing of a body; it lasts longer than re-frigeration, but not always as long as traditional embalming. Exactly how long depends on each particular circumstance, so consult a funeral director to discuss green embalming and your situation.

Be aware that not every funeral home believes in this new way of embalming, and not every funeral home car-ries these natural products. Some funeral providers believe wholeheartedly in traditional embalming and will try to push that service on indecisive family members. Be firm and ask for what you want, but do remember that no method of embalming allows a body to last forever. Use your own best judgment.

Handling the Body after Death

Washing and dressing the body yourself is a lovely tribute, an act of tenderness, and a sign of respect. Usually, those who were most involved in the person's physical care while they were alive may feel the most at ease contributing in this way.

If you plan to handle the body yourself at home, there are several considerations. The first is time. If burial will not occur within the first twenty-four hours after death, then the body will need some type of preservation, whether embalming or refrigeration (see page 109). Keep in mind that nursing homes and hospitals often want a body removed pronto, at any hour of the day or night, so you need to have your plan of preparation in place prior to death. If you have had a family death and are just reading this section now, go easy on yourself. Take a deep breath, and make the correct decision without feeling pressure.

A Word of Caution: Maintain a Sanitary Environment

If the loved one died at home, there will always be soiled items, such as sheets, clothes, and towels. If you prefer, you can choose to wear universal precautions — such as disposable latex gloves, protective clothing, and eye protection —

when handling these items or the deceased body. Most of the time this is unnecessary, unless you know the deceased had a blood-borne infection. Do try to avoid direct contact with blood or open sores, and practice thorough handwashing, both during and afterward, to minimize the risk of spreading infections or illness.

All nondisposable materials that the deceased came in contact with can be disinfected. A half cup of household bleach in a gallon of water is an effective disinfectant. Do not feel shameful if you need or want to throw everything out or burn it in a secured trash barrel or fireplace.

Rigor Mortis

All dead bodies undergo rigor mortis, which is a temporary stiffening of the joints and muscles that begins a few hours after death. Rigor mortis usually lasts for at least one day, but it can continue for up to three days or more. This medical condition sometimes makes maneuvering a body a bit problematic. If you can, make positioning easier by immediately doing so prior to rigor mortis setting in.

Here is a brief summary of the physical stages that occur in the days after death:

- During the first three hours after death: Body will be warm and flexible.
- Between three and eight hours after death: Body will remain warm to the touch, yet the limbs will begin to stiffen as rigor mortis sets in.
- Eight hours and perhaps up to seventy-two hours

after death: Body will become cold and remain stiff with rigor mortis.

- Anytime after thirty-six hours after death: Body will be cold, but muscles will relax; the body will no longer be stiff.
- Two or three days after death: Body will begin to putrefy if not preserved or embalmed.

Washing the Body

All dead bodies should be washed within a day after death. It's optimal to do so within minutes or hours after a loved one has passed away, since the skin will still be supple and warm to the touch, and the bathers will feel as if they are taking care of a sleeping person. Also, any unpleasant smells, feces, or fluids can be quickly whisked away from the body.

Freshening up the body is similar to a sponge bath. The attendants gently cleanse small areas at a time, and this allows the attendants quiet moments to gently position the body as they go. Always wash and work from head to toe. Moving and turning a dead body while washing can be awkward, so I recommend having a group of four to six people. Sometimes it is helpful to have even more people in the room for company and support; some can share stories of the loved one as others are directly hands-on with the bathing. Finally, create a loving ritual out of the act, with music, prayers, and positive memories. Lighting a candle is a really lovely way to begin the ritual.

You need to mentally prepare yourself to wash the nude

body of someone you love, which is uncharted territory for most people. Not only are you spending intimate time with someone you cared for, but they are no longer breathing. Their skin may be discolored, and there might be tubes and other devices attached to the body. Removing all of the clothing, bedding, diapers, and so on will make the washing process easier, but do this while remembering that continued reverence for the person's modesty is vital.

Most people feel more comfortable washing the body if the deceased's eyes are closed. You can do this gently with your gloved fingers, or you can rest a washcloth on the face.

As you begin and periodically throughout, everyone in the group should check in with one another. If, despite everyone's best intentions, someone finds the experience just too much to bear, allow them to excuse themselves. It is okay to feel overwhelmed. Equally, it is okay to deem one person the leader of the ritual if the others would rather take instruction during this unfamiliar journey.

As for supplies, all you need is a stack of washcloths and towels as well as a nearby bucket, bathtub, or sink basin filled with warm water and a small amount of soap. Don't use too much soap, as a small amount goes a long way in this process. If the hair of the deceased needs attention — such as a haircut or, for men, a shave — have those supplies ready as well.

As I advise, you might wish to wear protective gloves, smocks, or eyewear as you wash the deceased. As I've said, a dead body is not contagious, but your comfort and safety are key.

Once everything and everyone are in place, start the bath, including any ritual, music, prayers, or chanting you wish. Sometimes it's comforting to talk to the deceased as you work. I certainly do. In addition, it can be helpful if one person gives audible directions to the group, guiding everyone in what happens next.

As for the bath, start at the top of the head, and use a slightly dampened washcloth to slowly move around the face and down the front of the body. This is the time to trim a man's beard or give the person a haircut or a hair wash. If the mouth doesn't want to shut, do the teeth need to be brushed? If the mouth doesn't easily close, you can "tie" the mouth shut by placing a scarf or long piece of soft material under the jaw and making a bow at the top of the head. Once this is removed later, the mouth should remain closed.

Gingerly roll the person to each side, very slowly, to wash their back side. Use large-sized towels to pat dry as you move along. Treat the person as if they're alive to make this a somewhat more natural process. Eliminate all sheets or diapers as you bathe, but do replace them in order to help absorb any bodily fluid that might appear.

TIP: Prior to washing a body, make sure there is a container in the room to place dirty clothing and used items, which makes it easier to gather and haul away the soiled towels, bedding, sponges, and so on.

TALES FROM THE GRAVE

In ancient times, when coins were made out of heavier metals, coins were used to weight down the eyes of the deceased and allow them to shut. Ancient Greeks also put coins in the mouths of deceased people, believing they would have to pay the ferryman Charon to take them across the river Styx to the underworld.

Dressing the Body

After the body is washed, dress the deceased in what they will wear for burial. Since this is meant to be a green burial, avoid synthetic and non-natural materials. Of course, you may wish to adorn the person in appropriate or meaningful jewelry (it can be removed before burial if necessary), but choose clothing that reflects the green ethos of the burial itself.

Again, you might need several people for the task of lifting and positioning the body for dressing. Depending on how much time has passed since death, the body may be too limp or it might be less pliable than you want. To get a shirt or dress over the head and onto the body, gently work the arms into the sleeves first and then try to move the head through the top opening of the garment. If this won't work, consider cutting the garment along the back and tucking the sides under the body.

Once your deceased loved one is washed and dressed, move them to their coffin or to where they will be displayed for visitation. Place a pillow under their head and lay out the body in a natural-looking manner. Sometimes the visitation will take place where the person was bathed and dressed; they might have passed away in bed, and this could be the logical (or maybe the only) suitable place for them to receive visitors.

Refrigeration: Preserving the Body

After death, if no embalming is used, it is paramount to keep the body as cold as possible to slow decomposition. Most states have a funeral home rule that if final disposition does not occur within twenty-four hours, a body must be buried, cremated, embalmed, or refrigerated. Unless you are working with a funeral home, you probably will not have access to a refrigerator that can accommodate a body, so you can choose any cooling method at your disposal: dry ice, ice packs, air-conditioning, and so on. If it's winter, make sure the heat is off in the room where the body is kept; if it's summer, turn up the AC.

In my experience, if the ice is maintained consistently by changing it at least twice per day (and sometimes more), these cooling methods can successfully hold off decomposition for several days.

Besides the temperature of the air in the room, decomposition can occur at a faster rate depending on a few significant factors related to the deceased, such as if they are obese, have bed sores, or had high amounts of medication in their body when they passed away.

TIP: You might want to consider placing a thermometer in the casket or on the body to ensure you really are keeping the body cool enough.

Dry Ice

Dry ice, or frozen carbon dioxide, is the best substance to use if you don't have refrigeration. Dry ice is significantly colder than water ice, and it does not melt into a liquid; it evaporates, leaving behind virtually no mess.

Dry ice requires careful handling, you will need a lot of it, and it is a specialty item. To keep an average-sized body cool, I suggest surrounding the body with about twenty pounds of dry ice at a time. Since dry ice evaporates steadily, be prepared to purchase the same amount each day until burial.

This means you will need to identify a convenient dry ice supplier ahead of time, one that carries dry ice in sufficient quantities. All ice cream stores use dry ice, and some will sell it to the general public. You can also approach grocery stores and other retail stores (see the endnotes for further resources).

Most of all, you must be very careful handling dry ice, which is so cold that it can cause serious burns if touched. Always use thick leather or cloth gloves when handling dry ice, and store extra dry ice in an empty cooler (not in a conventional freezer, which can be damaged by it). Further, as dry ice evaporates, it emits carbon dioxide, which is of course toxic if it becomes too concentrated. Always make sure that you keep dry ice in well-ventilated areas. When transporting it in your car, keep the windows open, and make sure the room where the body is located has lots of fresh circulating air. If not, carbon dioxide fumes can pool, becoming dangerous and even deadly.

Finally, wrap small blocks of dry ice in cloths, and position them out of sight in a variety of places underneath the deceased's body. Place several bundles of dry ice along the back, which is the largest area, and then place other bundles under each arm and each leg. Check the dry ice regularly, such as every six hours, to make sure it hasn't evaporated and is performing as it should.

Another option is to use a "cooling blanket." These "blankets," made from a biodegradable material that looks like white plastic, can hold six small bricks of dry ice. The blankets can then be positioned around the body, even on top. Just lay a fabric blanket over the body, which improves insulation and looks nicer.

Reusable Ice Packs

If purchasing dry ice is not possible or feasible, then reusable ice packs can also be used (such as the Techni-Ice brand). As with dry ice, you will need a lot of these packs, which are also sold in connected sheets of a dozen. These can be refrozen in a conventional freezer, which is very helpful, and since they are self-contained and sealed, there is no water due to melting. However, they do create condensation, so you might want to place them in a breathable, absorbent pillowcase, towel, or other fabric. To use, place them around and underneath the body in the same manner as the dry ice.

Finally, if working with any type of ice is difficult or causes you stress, don't worry. Use the cooling technique you are most comfortable with, and if that means simply keeping the AC on a very low setting, you should be fine.

Transporting the Body

If you are not working with a funeral home and must transport the body long distances, particularly to another state, there are some issues to keep in mind.

Transporting a body across state lines is not complicated, but make sure you understand the rules in each state through which the body will travel. States do not have uniform laws, but they all have legal requirements, and these requirements occasionally change. For up-to-date information in a state-by-state chart, see the National Home Funeral Alliance's "Quick Guide to Legal Requirements for Home Funerals in Your State" (see the endnotes).

It is legal to transport a dead body in a personal vehicle. Any station wagon, minivan, truck bed with canopy, or large sport utility vehicle should work fine. Obviously, you need to measure the container holding the body to ensure that it will fit in your vehicle. It should go without saying that, during transportation, the dignity of the body should be preserved at all times, and that the container not impede the driver from safely operating the vehicle.

Finally, if embalming is not used, the body needs to be kept cold during transport. As mentioned above, dry ice is recommended, but how much you will need depends on the weather, the distance, and so on. If the trip is more than a few hours, stop to check on the ice and the body regularly. Families have told me the drive with their deceased loved one was much more relaxed when they had already located stores along their route that sell dry ice. Personally, I have used and recommend national ice cream shops like Baskin-Robbins, which will sell dry ice to the public in sufficient quantities and make a nice stop for a cool treat on a long, strange trip.

Chapter 9

CONDUCTING A HOME FUNERAL OR GREEN BURIAL

A resurgence in home funerals is rapidly growing across the country. With home funerals, families reclaim the personal sacredness of death and dying by taking a hands-on approach to some or all aspects of the funeral. Often, this provides families with the gifts of time, connection, and community, allowing everyone to celebrate and mourn together and in the ways they prefer.

As Lee Webster, president emeritus of the National Home Funeral Alliance, writes, "Home funerals are about empowering families to care for their own dead, to take the time to be present and absorb the loss, to complete a process that is intimate and meaningful without outsourcing it or parts of it unless desired, to build community around the loss of a member."

Humans certainly are not one-size-fits-all. We are a patchwork quilt of many ideas, beliefs, and life purposes. A home funeral and/or a green burial allow for lots of freedom when it comes to crafting the perfect, personalized event. Family-directed funerals encompass caring for dead loved ones (see chapter 8) and arranging some type of lovely, personalized send-off, one that emerges organically from open hearts.

In this chapter, I review some practical considerations related to the event, whether it will be a large community ceremony or a small, intimate gathering of quiet reflection, whether the burial is in your backyard or in a cemetery. However, please note that not all home funerals include a green burial, since many families choose cremation for their loved ones as the final method of disposition.

Planning the Ceremony

We spend our lifetimes searching for meaningful connections with others and creating lasting memories. This is a strong reason why we are moved to commemorate the end of a loved one's life. We give ourselves and our community a chance to remember them, to honor them, to mark that they were here with full hearts.

When planning the ceremony, the first question to ask is, what do you want to celebrate? Who was the person who died? What was their story, and what will be their legacy? And mostly, how did they want to be remembered?

The next of kin as well as any important decision makers from the guest of honor's tribe should meet to craft something personal and special. Who do you need to consult before making final decisions? Make sure to start conversations early with important family members.

Your celebration should reflect the wishes of the person who died, so consider how the event can celebrate their love of nature or sustainability, their religious or spiritual beliefs, and their life pursuits or passions. Families often cull ideas from prior services they've attended and creative websites such as Pinterest, and they draw inspiration from celebrations organized by their loved one when they were alive: What foods, decorations, colors, and music did they choose or gravitate toward? Don't forget to check the weather for the day chosen!

Then consider who will be coming: What are their expectations, religions, backgrounds, comfort levels, and so on? How will you accommodate and honor all other perspectives and attitudes? Is this event open to the public, will it be listed on social media, or is it more in line with your community to have just a small home funeral?

Here is a list of things you might include in a home funeral, along with brief explanations and options for each. For more thoughts on greening memorial services, see chapter 11. Also, please do not feel you need to incorporate everything in this list, as it might not be appropriate to your celebration:

A minister or leader? Does it feel correct for you to hire or appoint one person to be in charge, gather everyone's attention, or officiate? Would it be better for different people to lead at different points in the event?

Readings and prayers: Did the deceased have a favorite poet, author, songwriter, or Bible verse? Readings can be religious, spiritual, secular, or just some words reflecting their life. Maybe a special letter should be shared?

Music: Any songs or artists the decedent loved? Consider playing specific live or recorded songs during the service, or as possible background music before or after. Two to three selections tend to be what most people choose.

Speeches and eulogies: Has anyone offered to share the decedent's life story, their obituary, or stories about them? Would you like certain people to share certain information, or would you like to open the floor to anyone wanting to speak in front of the group?

Obituary or posting on social media: Most states do not have a rule that the public announcement needs to be made in print for all debtors and heirs, but a newspaper or online obituary is always an option. There is normally a cost and limited distribution associated with that method, so many people have started using email, Facebook, and other social media platforms to spread the word. Who will have the honor of gathering the information and writing the family obit?

Graveside ritual: Will there just be some words and the lowering of the body, or would you like to incorporate tossing flowers, photographs on a stand, writing letters, throwing dirt, releasing doves or biodegradable balloons, etc.?

Decorations: What physical items might help attendants to remember the person's life: poster boards with photos, a sign-in book with space for thoughts, significant objects from the person's life, a color theme, etc.

Viewing and visitation: Where will the visitation take place? How long will the service be? Will it be open to the public or only to invited guests? Some people are not interested in this option and prefer to have a closed casket or fully tied shroud where the body cannot be viewed yet people can physically be in its presence for closure.

Carpooling or guest transportation: Encourage guests to carpool or use ride shares to the visitation and the funeral. Put someone in charge of coordinating this. This helps make your funeral as green as the burial, and sharing transportation encourages people to share stories and make connections.

Donations, gifts, and receiving flowers: Have a basket or table ready for items that might be brought to the service by guests. Possibly offer an option besides flowers in announcements (see "Cut the Flowers," page 141).

Announcements and invitations: Will the funeral or burial information be delivered via phone or internet, or would you like to create something printed on recycled paper? Do you want to personalize this with a take-home gift for guests, such as "seed cards" as a green option?

Food: Are you looking at catering, a potluck, or a few people cooking? Maybe just some healthy

snacks and beverages? Any drinks? If you plan
to lay out a buffet spread, turn to "Sustainable
Mourning Meals," page 140.

Helpers: Do you need anyone to help clean, prepare,
build, or manage the space for the service? Do
you need to appoint anyone to lift, create, or
organize items? Call on your family and friends
who have offered to lend a hand.

Harry: Crafting His Own Casket

As examples of what green burials and home funerals can be
like, I want to share a couple of substantial, sustainable final
farewells that I had the pleasure to be involved with. Harry
was a most precious man who lived in my community. His
birthday came on a Wednesday; his wife, Mildred, invited
me over to talk about the reality of green options, which her
beloved Harry had read about in *Mother Jones* magazine.

Upon learning that a casket could be made out of any
organic matter, as long as it was able to bear the weight of its
occupant, Harry resolved to make his own casket prior to his
passing. Medical tests gave him about a year or so to see this
dream come true.

One day, Harry left his bed at the break of dawn, marched
out to the backyard, and using a kitchen cleaver, cut down a
large bushel of bamboo. He enlisted a son to help him thatch
a burial container that resembled a hope chest, in which
the bamboo was held together with straw and dried mud.
Harry's future casket spent plenty of time hardening in the
summer sun, then it lived in the garage through the soggy
fall.

Just before Halloween, Harry left the Earth. I joined his family at the house that evening. His daughter-in-law had baked his favorite peach pie, and his son helped me bathe and dress the man of the hour while we listened to Tony Bennett and Mel Tormé take turns singing in the living room.

Harry spent that evening in his self-made bamboo casket, right in the living room, as neighbors and former coworkers came by to say their good-byes. Outside, his two nephews were in the backyard bamboo grove, using a tractor to dig Harry's final resting space. They had borrowed the machinery from a neighbor, and one nephew already knew how to operate it. Fortunately, the grassy backyard was level, and the bamboo was quite pliable, which eased the nephews' work.

The family hired me to help ensure the backyard burial was legal in Clackamas County and followed county regulations. I contacted the county planning and zoning department to confirm the plot of land was considered rural. I also walked the area to look for any watersheds, make sure the grave was at least fifty feet away from the neighbor's home, and check for hardships, such as sinkholes or outcroppings of rock.

When Harry's grave was ready, the nephews and neighbors slowly carried him outside. At the graveside, everyone shared some laughs and some toasts, and then the casket was lowered. Simple and sweet, just like he was.

John: The Power of Music

John's death was imminent. He was in his early fifties and in the final stage of pancreatic cancer. The hospice nurse predicted he only had a few days left before he would be metaphorically crossing the road to see what was on the other side. Family members started arriving and took turns sitting next to his bed, holding his hand, and reassuring him with their presence that he would not die alone. They didn't know what else to do. The kitchen across the hall from the bedroom was overflowing with loved ones and good food. It served as a place of respite for John's many caregivers. Some days were quiet and sad; others were filled with storytelling as people reminisced with John.

Everyone was in the room the moment John drew his last shallow breath. The raggedy noise was followed by a deafening silence. No one moved for about fifteen minutes, until Jacob slipped out to fetch his guitar. Then we heard the almost angelic strains of "Tears in Heaven" by Eric Clapton. Everyone sat silently and Marielle recited a prayer. Someone brought in champagne from the kitchen, and everyone toasted John. Jacob kept playing music on his guitar: "For Emily, Whenever I May Find Her" by Simon and Garfunkel and then Bob Marley's "Redemption Song." Then John's mother read aloud the thoughts she had jotted down the previous night while sitting with John holding his hand. Everything happened organically and in perfect timing.

People started arriving, and Jacob kept playing songs on his guitar. John was sprayed with his favorite cologne, and with the help of two friends, he was nestled into a wool blanket his father had from army days. Stories, music, and love drifted all through the house as we waited for the call from the local gravedigger that they were ready for us to bring John.

The week prior, the family had visited the cemetery to

pick his burial spot, pay and sign the papers, and choose the boulder and inspirational quote that would serve as his grave marker. The family would have preferred a backyard burial on their own property, but this wasn't allowed where they live in Portland. However, they were at peace, since they felt John would have loved the small cemetery they selected for him, which had a designated green burial area.

Once the call from the cemetery came, the neighbors brought their Chrysler van (with the back seats down) up to the bedroom deck. Due to his medical treatments, John had become so shrunken that only two men were needed to carry him wrapped in his snug blanket. The music from the guitar set a lovely tone. The tender time was unceasing through the journey from the bedroom, out the sliding glass door, into the vehicle, and through the gates of the cemetery.

We stood in silence in the cemetery. It was all so natural and so very real. Nothing needed to be said. When the group felt ready, the sexton pushed the button on the lowering device to lower John into the grave. One by one, each person moved to the hole, peered in, and said their good-byes. As the group quietly left the graveyard in their vehicles, the sexton and I shoveled the soil into the grave as I shared with him how lovely the day had been with John and his community.

Planning the Burial

Not all home funerals end with a green burial. Many families opt for cremation or a standard, modern burial, so only consider the advice in this section that applies to your situation. However, whatever your plans, the central advice is to anticipate problems and be flexible as necessary. You may be fully devoted to realizing your vision, but sometimes weather, burial containers, and humans, whether dead or alive, can ruin your planned-to-the-letter event.

In addition to the emotional and spiritual aspects of funerals, there are always logistical and practical factors to consider: For instance, what's the weather forecast? What season is it? If you're holding a backyard burial, is the ground frozen or flooded and not suitable for digging? Have you anticipated every step of transporting your loved one from their deathbed to the gravesite? Do you have all the tools and equipment you need, and a backup plan if things change? If anyone will be upset by your and your loved one's wish to have a home funeral and a green burial, might they refuse to attend the service or could they hold up the burial if they don't agree with it?

What if the deceased is a bit of a trickster and decides to enjoy some mayhem at their final farewell?

Of course, you can't anticipate every problem. But here is a list of the things you should take care of prior to a loved one's death, to make sure that everything runs smoothly (or as smoothly as it can) when the time comes.

> **Paperwork:** Do you have a completed death certificate (and burial permit, if your state requires it)? Is there any will or legal documents that need to be located and read over?
> **Hired helpers:** Will you need a funeral director? A machine operator? An engineer?
> **Volunteer helpers:** Have you asked or assigned people to help with the service and handling the body?

Do you need pallbearers, gravediggers, drivers, a volunteer coordinator?

Cemetery: Has everything been paid for? Has the legal owner of the grave space signed the interment authorization? Does the driver know the best route to the cemetery? Have they done a dry run to check for current construction zones or any unknowns?

Backyard burial: Have you confirmed the suitability and legality of the gravesite? Has the exact space been decided on?

Transportation of the body: Do you have a vehicle, or can you borrow one? Have you confirmed the burial container fits in the vehicle? Who will drive and load the body into the vehicle? What is the plan for removing the body at the final destination?

Burial container: What do you plan to use? Do you have it ready? Who will act as pallbearers, and do they need instruction on how to handle the container? Do you need a lowering board or device under it?

Gravedigging plan: Do you have the necessary tools and helpers when it's time to dig? Have you inspected the soil and located any obstacles?

Unusual Gravesites and Trouble with Transport

As with ceremonies, I want to share a few stories about burials I've attended over the years. In this case, these snafus and hiccups provide useful lessons for anticipating and troubleshooting common problems that may also come up for you.

For instance, a family once approached me after their patriarch had passed away of natural circumstances in a hospital. The family didn't have a burial plan, and they asked me to place the man in refrigeration until they could decide what to do. Finally, they decided they would bury him out by his favorite fire pit in the backyard. However, the family didn't think through the logistics of their desired location, and getting there became an epic struggle.

The issue was maneuvering the deceased in his cardboard burial container from my vehicle all the way across the field to his burial space. The family knew the land wasn't suitable to drive over, and the man was too heavy, and the container too bulky, for people to carry. So they planned to use a rolling cart.

However, the cart wasn't long enough. The cardboard box was hanging off the back and threatening to collapse under its own weight. The family tried to enlist help from available neighbors to carry their loved one, but again, the cardboard container wasn't sturdy enough.

In my van, I had a church truck, which is an accordion-style folding aluminum rack that's used to transport caskets into a church. We decided to use this, since it could support the caskets and its heavy-duty wheels might manage the field. As we rolled about halfway across, everything seemed kosher. Then we hit a very sandy area. The heavy-duty tires sank, and the church truck became hopelessly stuck. The weight of the man and the casket sank the apparatus being used to propel him forward to the grave space.

Thankfully, it was early on a beautiful day with a clear blue sky, and some ingenious neighbors devised a towing mechanism with a riding lawnmower that successfully got the man where he needed to be, and he was buried without further obstacles.

Thinking back, I realize what would have been a better solution. We could have laid plywood to line our path. The even planking would have given the church truck a firm, clear surface for travel, and the wheels would have glided over, rather than sunk into, the sand. Also, the family could have arranged for a sufficiently large four-wheel-drive vehicle to successfully carry the casket across the sketchy, uneven field.

Looks Like Rain

A family was anticipating their mother's death, and they had done their homework for a backyard burial, marking the specific spot where they wanted to dig. They were justifiably proud of their organization. But as the end of their mother's life drew near, I had to be the bearer of bad news: The weather was taking a turn for the worse, and it looked as if freezing rain might be coming. I advised them to dig the grave now, ahead of the storm.

Of course, if they did, then the freshly dug grave might have filled with water and leaves, so I strategized how to place a tarp over the grave to protect it. However, the family eventually decided to wait a few more days to see what the weather would do. Sure enough, the mother died, the rain came, and the ground was frozen solid. Rather than hold the lovely service that the family had planned, they put their mother in refrigeration for a week waiting for the ground to thaw.

The opposite scenario happened to another family. Faced with impending rain, they predug the grave several days ahead of the burial. Rather than cover the open hole with a solid, rainproof tarp, however, they thought they could get away with just a net to keep the leaves out. They assumed the rainwater would be absorbed, and all would be easy peasy come burial time. Then it rained harder than expected, and the grave became a bit of a pond. They chose to use a sump pump to empty the rainwater rather than wait unknown hours for the water to slowly permeate the soil.

The lesson here is clear: *Always* watch the weather and be prepared. I know, I know. Easy to say, not so easy to do. Bad weather can impact our plans almost no matter what we do. However, these families would have saved themselves heartache and trouble if they had prepared for the worst rather than hoped for the best.

If you find yourself in the same situation, here's my advice: Go ahead and predig the grave. Then use a waterproof tarp (or two) to keep rain from filling the grave with water. If precipitation is light but winds are strong, you might use a net to keep leaves from filling up the space, or place plywood boards over it to stop dirt from blowing in. I once had a family pitch a tent over the open grave in order to protect the hole, as well as to protect their three dogs from falling in. (For more information and advice on grave maintenance, see the endnotes.)

Summertime Blues

Then there was the home funeral where it was way too hot inside, so the family opened the windows, but they didn't have screens, so the insects came in, making the viewing rather unpleasant.

During the warmer months, it is imperative that the room containing the body be as cool as possible. Make sure the room has a tight-fitting door that can fully close, and use an air-conditioning unit in the window or turn up the central AC. Fans can help, but they won't cool a space like air-conditioning. Especially if burial does not occur within the first twenty-four hours, a body needs to remain refrigeration-level cold to keep decomposition at bay for as long as possible. Again, up to a few days is normally what you can expect before the body wants to naturally break down.

Practice Makes Perfect

During home funerals, people are often doing things they've never done before, and unfortunately, they sometimes learn the hard way — through mistakes. I remember one funeral where the shroud covering the deceased wasn't tied securely, and regrettably, it came loose, exposing Grandma in her birthday suit to everyone at the service.

Oh, dear! This was so tragically sad. If you are using a shroud, blanket, sheet, or really, doing anything for the first time, practice before the time comes. Do a dry run, and check that caskets fit through doorways and into vehicles. Practice tying a shroud on the living so that you don't have to figure it out in the moment, when emotions are high. If nothing else, this provides a unique and unusual experience you'll never forget.

Chapter 10

CREMATION

Traditional cremation is certainly on the rise in all areas of the United States and Canada, yet it is not an environmentally friendly process, and it's not considered a form of green burial. As I discuss in chapter 1 (see "Cremation: Ashes to Ashes Doesn't Always Mean Green," page 24), traditional cremation creates fossil-fuel emissions, and the ashes themselves can contain toxins. However, a new green method of cremation is rising in popularity, and there are certainly a number of creative and eco-friendly ways to preserve one's "cremains," as they are called.

Alkaline Hydrolysis

The process called alkaline hydrolysis — also known as water resomation, bio-cremation, and flameless cremation — uses heat, lye, and water to dissolve or break down a human body into liquid and some remaining bone.

Dean Fisher, who heads UCLA's Body Donation Program, says this process works with a light carbon footprint "because it catalyzes the hydrogen in water to more rapidly attack the chemical bonds between molecules in the body."

Alkaline hydrolysis is generally done in a large stainless-steel cylinder, with a person's former life vehicle amounting to a coffee-colored liquid that can be safely disposed of down a drain. The remaining bone fragments are ground into a powder and given to the family, much like a traditional cremation.

While costs vary, alkaline hydrolysis typically costs $150 to $500 more than traditional cremation. Otherwise, this is the clear green choice. For instance, the Sierra Club writes, "Lower temperatures help reduce carbon emissions; alkaline hydrolysis's emissions are just 10 to 15 percent of cremation's." The table below compares the carbon emissions of traditional cremation to those of alkaline hydrolysis.

TRADITIONAL CREMATION VS. ALKALINE HYDROLYSIS: CARBON FOOTPRINT COMPARISON

	Traditional	vs.	Alkaline Hydrolysis
Container Production	28		3
Fuel Consumption	201		25
Electrical Consumption	10		7
NOx Emissions	3		
Other Emissions	1		1
KOH Production / Transport			16
CH$_4$/NOx from Water Processing			4
Energy at Processing Plant			3
Total kg CO$_2$ Equivalents	**243**		**59**
			= 75.72% less carbon impact on environment

(credit: Sandy Sullivan, Resomation, Inc.)

Dr. Billy Campbell, steward of Ramsey Creek Preserve, the first noted US green burial ground, has researched the process of resomation and found that it occurs naturally when a body is buried in neutral or slightly alkaline soil. He writes, "To a great extent the bodies are decomposed by alkaline hydrolysis, expedited by soil bacteria and it is a very slow process."

As of early 2018, twelve US states consider alkaline hydrolysis a legal form of body disposition: California, Colorado, Florida, Georgia, Idaho, Illinois, Kansas, Maine, Maryland, Minnesota, Oregon, and Wyoming. Two Canadian provinces are also on board. If you prefer cremation to burial, consider choosing this more gentle and green process instead.

Creative Cremains

Like cremation, alkaline hydrolysis results in ashes that families must either dispose of or keep. As I mention earlier, if you want to spread a loved one's ashes, always check the laws of the state where you want to spread the ashes. Laws vary, and it will help your closure to know you aren't breaking any rules.

Cremains can be buried in a backyard, in a traditional cemetery plot, or in special burial areas called EcoEternity Forests. These are burial grounds located in several states that have small placements for biodegradable urns. A family can lease a tree for their loved one and have a small plaque attached to it with an inscription for the buried remains.

If you will be keeping the ashes, here are some creative options to consider besides the traditional ceramic or metal urn.

Dryer Lint Urns

When my daughter was quite small, I noticed that all our dryer lint became bright and colorful. Her girly clothing left behind something magical, and I knew I should lay it out for birds to make nests or store it away as a fire starter on camping trips. Or maybe I could give it to my funeral families to organically wrap portions of their loved one's cremains.

In 2010, as the fortieth anniversary of Earth Day was approaching, I decided to see if I could fabricate cremation urns out of all the lint I had set aside. I soon realized I could scoop out the clingy bits of fiber and fluff and create sustainable art.

A local artist friend, Marliese Franklin, and I sautéed the lint in water in a large saucepan, stirring well. Slowly adding flour, we cooked my dryer dust dregs over medium heat, rousing constantly until the mixture held together, forming peaks. We then poured it out onto several layers of newspaper to cool.

Dryer lint urns have two obvious advantages: They are environmentally friendly, as one would expect a biodegradable urn to be, and you can make them essentially for free. They are a natural demonstration of the cycle of life — we are born, we die, we replenish the Earth, and the cycle begins again — as well as a great option for anyone on a budget.

I gave away the urns I made for free to anyone in need who wanted one, and I encourage you to try making your own, using my simple recipe:

- 3 cups dryer lint
- 2 cups warm water
- 1 cup flour

Environmentally friendly, biodegradable urn made out of dryer lint (Photo credit: Elizabeth Fournier)

When I ran out of my own lint, I called a local laundromat, which happily donated twenty pounds for a good cause. For families stressed by personal loss and the high costs of an average funeral, every little bit of savings can help.

Eternal Reefs

How about spending eternity at the bottom of the ocean? In a way, this is like burial at sea, only with cremation ashes.

The Georgia-based company Eternal Reefs takes human ashes and mixes them with cement to create "reef balls." Looking like large Whiffle balls, these cast structures are sunk offshore and become artificial reefs for fish and other marine life. Though the reef balls don't decay, they still support a sustainable ocean, and the location of each specific reef ball in the ocean can be located using GPS.

Bio Urns

Several companies now offer something called a bio urn, which is a biodegradable urn that contains the seed or sapling of a tree. Customers can typically choose the tree of their choice (ideally one that will thrive in their particular location), and once planted, your or a loved one's ashes will always be marked, not by a headstone, but by a tree.

Note that in these products, the tree roots don't grow directly in the dense cremains, which are usually lower in the basket. See the endnotes for resources.

Let Your Love Grow

As I mentioned, undiluted cremains are not healthy for plants, so the company Let Your Love Grow has solved this problem by mixing human cremation ash with a specially formulated organic mixture so that cremains can be used as planting soil. This mixture contains a very low sodium and pH content, which allows the ashes to release only nutrients that will fertilize plants.

Sustainable Art: Rest in Pieces

Artist Nadine Jarvis's designs have turned cremation ashes into bird feeders, pencil boxes, and other concepts of rebirth.

For one piece, Jarvis created a set of 240 pencils from human ash, cleverly called the Carbon Copies, each embossed with the name and dates of the person. A special pencil box allows only one pencil to be removed from the box at a time, and a built-in sharpener collects the pencil shavings, which really are carbon remnants of human remains. As the pencils are used, the box becomes an urn, holding the person's remains. Of course, this isn't an actual product you can buy, but it shows how a little creativity can lead to unique, "sustainable" remembrances of those you love.

For instance, I know a woman who, after her fiftieth birthday, had a midlife mortality crisis. Instead of trembling and moaning, she decided to make art. She sent out word to all her family and friends: Anyone who had metal orthopedic parts, and who desired cremation, should leave those parts to her. This became her way of celebrating both their lives and life itself. Turns out, her cousin had once swallowed some tiny screws back in high school as a dare. They remained in his body at death, and yep, she now has them framed. What a wonderful way to remember him! The woman has also made wind chimes out of titanium hip replacement pieces, and she now keeps the memory of those friends alive through the songs of their "bones."

I also once read of a grandson who collected the metallic pieces from his grandfather's cremated remains, polished them up, put them on a plaque, and labeled it: Grandpa. What a great conversation piece!

Chapter 11

A GREEN GOODBYE

Memorials and Mementos

T his chapter speaks to those who are planning a funeral as well as to those who are guests at a funeral. Whether a burial is meant to be "green" or not, you can still make eco-friendly, sustainable choices, such as with the food served and the gifts and mementos given and shared (for more on funeral planning, see chapter 9). At some point, we all will attend a funeral for someone we know and love, so let's make these "green good-byes."

Have you heard of the term "shades of green"? I like this compassionate term because it gives us permission to do the best we can without feeling that we failed for not being able to deliver a 100-percent green funeral or burial. Ultimately, I hope that this book inspires you to consider what you want your end-of-life arrangements to be and to have the "talk of a lifetime" with those you love. I hope that includes a green burial and the desire to have your send-off and final rest support natural, sustainable processes.

Whatever you decide, start now. Express those wishes to the people who most likely will have to carry them out. Work on a plan, revise the plan, place all the details in a bright-colored notebook, and let people know where you keep that notebook. Be brave and make it happen.

Sustainable Mourning Meals

When people come to show their respect, they often descend upon the grieving household with their favorite prepared casserole. One way anyone can help a family in mourning is to feed them. Food is comfort, but we should ensure that the food we bring fosters sustainability as well.

Traditionally, women prepared funeral feasts that made the day — great amounts of soup, casseroles, aspics, Virginia ham, cold cuts, potato salad, deviled eggs, pound cakes, and so on. Wakes meant lots of basic "mom is here to take care of you" food for a wearisome day. This remains true in many places, though we can revise the menu and how these buffets are managed to minimize waste. At minimum, assign someone to help sort the trash into what's recyclable, what's reusable, and what's compostable. If lots of food remains by the end of the event, and the family cannot eat it all, make sure people leave with the leftovers. Maybe even encourage your guests to bring their own take-home container if you feel this will be the case.

If you're planning a funeral, assign someone to coordinate food and gifts and perhaps set up a schedule for gift meals, so they arrive over time and not all at once. Some people call this a meal train, which can be emailed out as an electronic calendar. Volunteers sign up for when and what they would like to bring to the family.

If you're bringing food, make it healthy food made with fresh, sustainably grown ingredients — use meat from humanely raised cattle with no added hormones or antibiotics. Use fresh produce that is chemical-free, pesticide-free, and grown locally whenever possible. If you can, make homemade dishes, rather than bring store-bought ones. But if you buy prepared foods, avoid those with additives, preservatives, lard, canola oil, gluten, and trans fat. Also consider sustainable plates, bowls, flatware, and cups.

TIP: If you want to bring a food gift, consider a big pot of nutritious soup. The family can leave it simmering on the stove and dip into it when the mood suits.

Cut the Flowers

Flowers can be a very large expense at funerals. A traditional casket blanket of flowers or a standing floral display can cost many hundreds of dollars. If you're planning a funeral, some money-saving ideas include using artificial flowers or having potted plants rather than cut and arranged flowers. Or skip the flowers entirely. I have seen lovely casket toppers that didn't use flowers at all, such as surrounding a framed photograph of the departed loved one with a wreath made from branches, ribbons, and even a favorite clothing item. I've seen this done with a skateboard and tennis shoes, and a cowboy could be celebrated by displaying his hat, boots, and lead rope.

For ornamental flair and color, top the casket with a homemade or special blanket. For deceased military veterans, obtain a flag from their branch of service, and cover the casket with it. Before burial, this can be folded and presented to the next of kin.

Another reason to avoid cut flowers is that they have a high environmental cost. Not only are many cut flowers imported from other countries (all those plane flights involve lots of greenhouse-gas emissions), but they are also laden with pesticides and are carted around in energy-guzzling refrigerated trucks and display cases. If you are a guest at a funeral, choose another way to honor the deceased than by sending an expensive floral arrangement that will, in a few days, only become landfill.

> TIP: If you are planning a funeral, ask mourners to make donations to a favorite charity in honor of the deceased rather than send floral tributes. Or ask others to plant a tree, and so honor the person's life by fostering more life.

Seed Cards: Plantable Thank-You Notes

Seed cards are made from completely biodegradable natural fibers that are embedded with plantable seeds. These cards can be used a myriad of ways. I have had families use them to write thank-you notes to those who attended a memorial service or burial or as a gift for friends who went out of their way to assist in a time of need. These cards can also be used as a keepsake from the service. Some seed cards are made from recycled paper, some can be personalized, and some are shaped into remembrance ornaments. However, whatever the style, they can be kept as a keepsake or planted and cared for till the plants, often wildflowers, germinate and grow, blooming into a living memorial (see the endnotes for resources). You might consider holding a special planting ceremony, either using the seed cards or just having family and friends gather after the funeral to create a memorial garden. And don't forget: Choose seeds for plants that are native to your region.

Recycled-Paper Memory Cards

Memory cards are small pieces of paper that are usually handed out to funeral guests as they enter the visitation or service, and on which everyone writes sweet thoughts and memories of the deceased loved one. Sometimes the cards are read at the service; other times they are saved to be read and shared at a later date. Either way, they create a special opportunity for people to share emotions and happy memories. For instance, I know a family who brings out the handwritten memorial tributes each Christmas when the house is full of relatives, and they take turns reading them and placing each one on the Christmas tree in honor of their grandmother.

If you are planning a funeral, I recommend using them, and if you do, choose ones made with recycled paper and eco-friendly ink. Even memories should be sustainable!

Biodegradable Dove Balloons

Many times at gravesite ceremonies, mourners will release helium balloons or live doves to symbolize the freedom of the human spirit as well as the physical and emotional act of letting go of the person who has passed. Releasing balloons is a moving gesture, until of course the balloons eventually fall and become trash. For a sustainable option, use biodegradable, helium "dove" balloons, which can float for nearly twenty hours in the sky. The biodegradable material quickly breaks down with help from the sun and water (see the endnotes for resources).

Sharing Treasures

As they say, you can't take it with you. Deceased loved ones leave their things behind, and these can sometimes be used as loving mementos in themselves. For instance, a dear friend of mine became a widower suddenly when his wife, Janelle, died on her way to work. Janelle's heart gave out close to their neighborhood, and my friend found her looking peaceful in her truck, which had slowly rolled to a stop on the side of a quiet street. At her memorial service later that weekend, all the guests were instructed to choose a scarf from the collection laid out across the bed in a spare room. Janelle loved scarves, and her family felt giving away one of her favorite things was an appropriate way to honor those who were coming to pay tribute to her. At the celebration of Janelle's life, everyone held this loving tribute, many tucked around their necks. Later, they took their precious treasure home to wear in memory of their dear, departed friend. Sustainability at its finest!

ACKNOWLEDGMENTS

Thanks to...

My mother, who was inspired by Anne Frank's desire to breathe in nature any chance she could. In turn, she passed that gift on to me. When I was a very small child, my mother loved to read a passage written by Anne in her diary: "The best remedy for those who are afraid, lonely or unhappy is to go outside, somewhere where they can be quiet, alone with the heavens, nature and God. Because only then does one feel that all is as it should be and that God wishes to see people happy, amidst the simple beauty of nature."

My father, who was a wonderful human, my greatest fan, and a central character in my prior books. How perfectly fitting that he slipped away from Earth while I wrote this one.

My husband, Michael, who with the patience of a calm current holds my hand as I walk my journey, and my daughter, Sofia, who inspires me with her sense of wonder and her concern for nature's creatures.

My editors, Jason Gardner and Jeff Campbell, who championed my green burial passion and worked so diligently to shape my thoughts into a comprehensible guidebook.

My literary agent, Adria Goetz, a true Proverbs 31 woman.

And a very loving embrace to the families who are hurting due to the death of someone they love in this present moment. Please know that you are not alone.

ENDNOTES

Introduction

Page 1, *"Death is an integral part of life"*: Elisabeth Kübler-Ross, *Death: The Final Stage of Growth* (New York: Touchstone, 1986), 5.

Page 3, *Green burial is a way of caring for our dead*: Joe Sehee, "What Is Green Burial?" Green Burial Council, https://greenburialcouncil.org/home/what-is-green-burial.

Chapter 1. Green Burial, the Funeral Industry, and the Environment

Page 13, *While mummification and embalming were known*: K. D. Pryor, *When a Loved One Dies* (Ann Arbor, MI: Kaleidoscope Books, 2011), 69.

Page 14, *In the most familiar definition, a green burial means a person*: "Green Funerals and Burial," National Funeral Directors Association, http://www.nfda.org/consumer-resources/planning-a-funeral/green-funerals-and-burial, 2017.

Page 14, *However, there are also dedicated green cemeteries and "green burial sites"*: Tanja L. Schade, "The Green Cemetery in America: Plant a Tree on Me" (master's thesis, Evergreen State College, June 2011), http://archives.evergreen.edu/masterstheses/Accession86-10MES/Schade_TMES thesis2011.pdf.

Page 15, *A home funeral can include all of the elements of a customary funeral*: Joy Jernigan, "More Families Are Bringing Funerals Home," *NBC News,* September 24, 2007, http://www.nbcnews.com/id/20845739/ns/health-behavior/t/more-families-are-bringing-funerals-home.

Page 15, *"You can also find a funeral home, with a refrigeration unit"*: "Choosing Green or Natural Burial," Seven Ponds, http://www.sevenponds.com /after-death/choosing-green-burial-or-natural-burial.

Page 19, *The Centers for Disease Control and Prevention makes it clear that the average dead body:* "Dead Bodies and Disease: The 'Danger' That Doesn't Exist," Funeral Consumers Alliance, January 30, 2008, https://funerals. org/embalming -myths-facts.

Page 20, *As Suzanne Kelly writes in* Greening Death*: "Newly trained civilian":* Suzanne Kelly, *Greening Death: Reclaiming Burial Practices and Restoring Our Tie to the Earth* (Lanham, MD: Rowman & Littlefield, 2015), 41.

Page 21, *After President Lincoln was assassinated, the way his body:* Alvin J. Schmidt, *Cremation, Embalmment, or Neither? A Biblical/Christian Evaluation* (Bloomington, IN: WestBow Press, 2015).

Page 22, *Today, as Jessica Mitford illuminated in her 1963 bestseller:* Richard Severo, "Jessica Mitford, Incisive Critic of American Ways and a British Upbringing, Dies at 78," *New York Times,* July 24, 1996, http://www .nytimes.com/1996/07/24/arts/jessica-mitford-incisive-critic-american -ways-britishupbringing-dies-78.html.

Page 22, *How squeamish are Americans about death? We are the country:* Barry Sanders, *Unsuspecting Souls: The Disappearance of the Human Being* (Berkeley, CA: Counterpoint Press, 2009), 107.

Page 23, *"The typical ten-acre swath of cemetery ground":* Mark Harris, *Grave Matters* (New York: Scribner, 2007), 38.

Page 23, *Katrina Spade, founder of Recompose, writes:* Katrina Spade, "How Your Death Affects Climate Change," *Huffington Post,* December 3, 2014, last updated February 2, 2015, https://www.huffingtonpost.com/katrina -spade/how-your-death-affects-cl_b_6263152.html.

Page 23, *To quantify these impacts with slightly different numbers:* Mary Woodsen, "Why Choose Green Burial," *Greensprings Natural Cemetery, March 2007,* http://www.naturalburial.org/why-choose-green-burial.

Page 24, *"we bury enough embalming fluid to fill eight Olympic-sized":* Cheryl Corley, "Burials and Cemeteries Go Green," *NPR Radio,* December 16, 2007, http://www.npr.org/templates/story/story.php?storyId=17232879.

Page 24, *According to a 2016* Time *magazine report, only about 10 percent of people:* Josh Sanborn, "Cremation Is Now Outpacing Traditional Burial in the

U.S.", *Time*, August 1, 2016, http://time.com/4425172/cremation-outpaces-burial-u-s.

Page 25, *Typically, cremation ovens use fossil fuels, and they must maintain:* Nina Rastogi, "The Green Hereafter," *Slate*, February 17, 2009, http://www .slate.com/articles/health_and_science/the_green_lantern/2009/02 /the_green_hereafter.html.

Page 25, *The United Nations estimates that crematoriums contribute:* "Agriculture's Greenhouse Gas Emissions on the Rise, Warns UN Agency," *UN News Centre*, April 11, 2014, http://www.un.org/apps/news/story .asp?NewsID=47563#.WgCYAiMrInU.

Page 25, *Cremation ashes are primarily tricalcium phosphate:* Sarah Tarlow and Liv Nilsson Stutz, *The Oxford Handbook of the Archaeology of Death & Burial* (Oxford, UK: Oxford University Press, 2013), 150.

Page 26, *If you want to scatter cremains or bury them, follow the advice:* Gail Rubin and Susan Fraser, *Celebrating Life: How to Create Meaningful Memorial Services with Templates & Tips* (March 2015), https://www.inthelighturns .com/Celebrating-Life-How-To-Create-Meaningful-Memorial-Services.pdf.

Chapter 2. Green Burial Practices: Yesterday, Today, and Tomorrow

Page 28, *green burial "is a way for families to talk about resurrection":* Lauren Markoe, "Green Burials Reflect a Shift to Care for the Body and Soul," *Washington Post*, January 23, 2014, https://www.washingtonpost.com /national/religion/green-burials-reflect-a-shift-to-care-for-the-body-and -soul/2014/01/23/169a359a-8470-11e3-a273-6ffd9cf9f4ba_story.html.

Page 28, *According to Maria Margiotta, "Before the development of chemical":* Maria Margiotta, "'Green' Burial in the Catholic Tradition," *Catholic Cemetery*, July 2016, http://www.rcancem.org/wp-content/uploads/2016/07 /JULY_Catholic-Cemetery-Magazine.pdf.

Page 28, *Father Charles Morris — who oversees Mount Carmel Cemetery:* Rich Heffern, "Lay Your Loved Ones to Rest the Natural Way," *National Catholic Reporter*, April 21, 2009, https://www.ncronline.org/news/lay-your -loved-ones-rest-natural-way.

Page 29, *According to the website Funeralwise, "Jewish funeral traditions require":* "Naturally Green Jewish Burial Rituals," FuneralWise, https://www.funeral wise.com/customs/green_jewish.

Page 29, *Traditional Islamic burial practice states that the deceased loved one:*

Clifton D. Bryant, *Handbook of Death and Dying* (Thousand Oaks, CA: Sage Publications, 2003), 650–51.

Page 30, *I had the honor to serve as funeral director for a Native American burial:* This story is adapted from a previous publication: Elizabeth Fournier, "Sacred Medicine Wheel," Naturally Savvy, April 12, 2012, http://naturally savvy.com/live/sacred-medicine-wheel.

Page 31, *If you visit the Philippines, head to the northern city of Sagada:* "Hanging Coffins," Wikipedia, https://en.wikipedia.org/wiki/Hanging_coffins.

Page 32, *In the high mountains of Tibet, with hard ground and little wood:* Seth Faison, "Lirong Journal; Tibetans, and Vultures, Keep Ancient Burial Rite," *New York Times,* July 3, 1999, http://www.nytimes.com/1999/07 /03/world/lirong-journal-tibetans-and-vultures-keep-ancient-burial-rite .html.

Page 32, *Ken West, who was the bereavement services manager of the Carlisle:* Cynthia Beal, "Sustainable Cemetery Management — Revitalizing Exist- ing Cemeteries," *American Cemetery Magazine,* March 2009, http://www .beatree.com/2009/05/sustainable-cemetery-management.html.

Page 32, *In the United States, one of the first natural burial grounds:* Chuck Hall, *Green Circles: A Sustainable Journey from the Cradle to the Grave* (Seattle: CreateSpace, 2013), 136.

Page 33, *In 2012, the United Kingdom had more than 250 green burial sites:* Cynthia Beal, "Natural Burial; the Ultimate Back-to-the-Land Move- ment," *Be a Tree: The Natural Burial Guide for Turning Yourself into a Forest,* http://beatree.com.

Page 33, *To quote the official website: "At a Death Cafe":* "What Is Death Cafe?" DeathCafe.com, http://deathcafe.com/what.

Page 34, *As quoted in* People *magazine, Rory wrote that:* Maria Mercedes Lara, "Joey Feek Dead: Rory Feek on Her Funeral," *People,* March 13, 2016, http://people.com/country/joey-feek-dead-rory-feek-on-her-funeral.

Page 35, *In 2010, British actress Lynn Redgrave's body was laid to rest:* "Vanessa Redgrave Says Final Goodbye to Sister Lynn as Family Gathers for Con- necticut Funeral," *Daily Mail,* May 8, 2010, http://www.dailymail.co.uk /tvshowbiz/article-1275324/Lynn-Redgrave-funeral-Vanessa-Liam -Neeson-mourners.html.

Page 35, *According to reports on CNN, television legend Andy Griffith:* "Andy Griffith Buried Shortly after Death, Source Says," *CNN,* July 3, 2012,

http://www.cnn.com/2012/07/03/us/north-carolina-griffith-burial
/index.html.

Page 35, *Civil rights leader and founder of the United Farm Workers (UFW):*
Frank Bardacke, "Cesar's Ghost," *The Nation,* January 21, 2006,
https://www.thenation.com/article/cesars-ghost.

Page 36, *"Ancient Vikings lit funeral pyres…day before the ceremony":* Ivan
Moreno, "Funeral Pyres an Option in Colorado Mountain Town,"
Associated Press, February 1, 2011, https://www.washingtontimes.com
/news/2011/feb/1/funeral-pyres-an-option-in-colorado-mountain-town.

Page 37, *They are formally known as "forensic anthropology research facilities":*
Tom Scheve, "How Body Farms Work," How Stuff Works, June 18, 2008,
https://science.howstuffworks.com/body-farm.htm.

Page 37, *In Australia (and a few other places), vertical burials:* "Standing the Dead
to Rest at Australia's Upright Cemetery," Funeral Zone, January 26, 2017:
https://www.funeralzone.com.au/blog/upright-burials.

Page 38, *Swedish biologist Susanne Wiigh-Mäsak has been developing*: Peter Vin-
thagen Simpson, "Swedes Told to Bury 'Freeze-Dried' Dead," *The Local
Sweden,* April 23, 2013, https://www.thelocal.se/20130424/47524.

Page 39, *The Capsula Mundi pods will be entirely organic:* Paula Erizanu, "The
Biodegradable Burial Pod That Turns Your Body into a Tree," *CNN,*
May 3, 2017, http://www.cnn.com/2017/05/03/world/eco-solutions
-capsula-mundi/index.html.

Page 39, *Recompose is the brainchild of Washington:* Brendan Kiley, "Seattle
Could Get an Urban Death Project Human Composter in Just 7 Years,"
Seattle Times, last updated October 31, 2016, https://www.seattletimes
.com/life/from-corpse-to-compost-the-urban-death-projects-modest
-proposal.

Chapter 3. Making a Plan: Green Burials and Home Funerals

Page 43, *"The reality is that you will grieve forever":* Elisabeth Kübler-Ross, *On
Grief and Grieving: Finding the Meaning of Grief through the Five Stages of
Loss* (New York: Scribner, 2007), 230.

Page 43, *"While more than nine in ten Americans think it's important to talk":* "A
Conversation with Ellen Goodman about the Conversation Project," Stan-
ford School of Medicine, https://aging.stanford.edu/2013/11/talking
-ellen-goodman.

Page 45, *Traditionally, the Irish celebrate the deceased at home:* "Weird Funeral

and Burial Practices," Nerdy Gaga, July 28, 2011, http://www.nerdygaga
.com/4155/weird-funeral-and-burial-practices.

Page 46, *Few in America currently care for their dead at home, but the number is
increasing:* Katie Zezima, "Home Burials Offer an Intimate Alternative,"
New York Times, July 20, 2009, http://www.nytimes.com/2009/07/21
/us/21funeral.html.

Page 48, *An average estimate of a modern funeral and burial:* "How Much Does
the Average Funeral Cost?" Parting.com, January 23, 2017, https://www
.parting.com/blog/how-much-does-the-average-funeral-cost.

Page 51, *The "Funeral Rule" of the Federal Trade Commission:* "The FTC Funeral
Rule," Federal Trade Commission, July 2012, https://www.consumer.ftc
.gov/articles/0300-ftc-funeral-rule.

Chapter 4. Legalities to Consider

Page 55, *However, as of 2017, ten states require you to appoint a funeral:* "Your
Funeral Rights," Funeral Consumers Alliance, https://funerals.org
/?consumers=your-funeral-rights.

Page 56, *Here is what these states require, as described by:* Lee Webster and Josh
Slocum, *Restoring Families' Right to Choose: The Call for Funeral Legislation
Change in America* (Seattle, WA: CreateSpace Independent Publishing
Platform, 2016), a publication of the National Home Funeral Alliance
and the Funeral Consumers Alliance. In addition, this list of states can
be found on the National Home Funeral Alliance's website, under "Ten
Restrictive States" (http://homefuneralalliance.org/the-law/problem
-states) and "Quick Guide to Legal Requirements for Home Funerals in
Your State" (http://homefuneralalliance.org/the-law/quick-guide).

Page 58, *According to USLegal.com, "State legislatures have adopted":* "Dead
Bodies," USLegal.com, https://deadbodies.uslegal.com.

Page 59, *To qualify as next of kin, a person must be over eighteen:* For a comprehensive list of next of kin, see "Next of Kin," Wikipedia, https://en
.wikipedia.org/wiki/Next_of_kin.

Page 62, *As an example, the Oregon home funeral packet contains:* "Matters of
Record," Oregon State Vital Records, July 2014. Note that the Oregon
home funeral packet isn't available online; it's mailed when requested with
a telephone call.

Chapter 5. It Takes a Village: Getting Help and Hiring Professionals

Page 69, *The Green Burial Council defines greenwashing:* Lee Webster, *Changing Landscapes: Exploring the Growth of Ethical, Compassionate, and Environmentally Sustainable Green Funeral Service* (Seattle, WA: CreateSpace Independent Publishing Platform, Green Burial Council International, 2017), 129.

Page 70, *"Like birth, death is one of life's most important":* Richard Gunderman, "Midwives for the Dying," *The Atlantic*, December 16, 2013, https://www.theatlantic.com/health/archive/2013/12/midwives-for-the-dying/282344.

Page 70, *an end-of-life doula can provide emotional, psychological, and spiritual support:* For more information, visit the National End-of-Life Doula Alliance (NEDA), http://www.nedalliance.org/about.html.

Page 71, *Cassandra Yonder calls death midwifery "a grassroots":* Cassandra Yonder, "Beyond Yonder," Death Midwifery, http://www.deathmidwifery.ca/death_death_midwifery.html.

Page 71, *Another important role in the death-care continuum:* Lee Webster, "Clearly Defined: Matching Our Terminology to Our Intentions," *National Home Funeral Alliance*, http://homefuneralalliance.org/resources/what-are-we-called.

Page 71, *According to Lee Webster, founding member of the National End-of-Life Doula Alliance:* Lee Webster, email correspondence with author, January 27, 2018.

Page 72, *Nancy Ward, who runs Sacred Endings in Scappoose:* Megan Brescini, "Women of Death," *Willamette Week*, May 19, 2009, http://www.wweek.com/portland/article-10563-women-of-death.html.

Chapter 6. A Place to Rest: Green Cemeteries and Backyard Burials

Page 74, *"The use of outer burial containers or vaults":* "Green Funerals and Burial," National Funeral Directors Association, http://www.nfda.org/consumer-resources/planning-a-funeral/green-funerals-and-burial.

Page 74, *The Green Burial Council distinguishes three types:* "Cemetery Certification Standards," Green Burial Council, March 6, 2015, http://greenburialcouncil.org/wp-content/uploads/2015/07/2015CemStandards.pdf.

Page 76, *Williamsburg Cemetery in Kitchener, Ontario, boasts beautiful:*

Williamsburg Cemetery, City of Kitchener Cemeteries, http://www
.kitchenercemeteries.ca/en/ourcemeteries/Williamsburg_Cemetery.asp.

Page 79, *In essence, private property burial is often allowed:* P. Fracone, "Can I Be
Buried on Private Property?" MySendOff.com, https://mysendoff
.com/2011/12/can-i-be-buried-on-private-property.

Page 79, *I've read other regulations that stipulate that private burial sites:* "Issues
to Consider in Preparing for Disposition of Decedents," Mass.gov,
http://www.mass.gov/eohhs/gov/departments/dph/programs
/environmental-health/comm-sanitation/burial-and-cremation.html.

Page 80, *"If you bury a body on private land, you should draw":* Sami Grover, "The
Dirt on DIY Funerals: What Is Legal?" Mother Nature Network, December 6, 2017, https://www.mnn.com/lifestyle/responsible-living/stories
/legality-diy-funerals.

Page 80, *According to the website Funeral Helper, "Heavy clay soils":* "Garden
Burial," Funeral Helper, http://www.funeralhelper.org/garden-burial.html.

Page 81, *According to* Mental Floss *magazine, the phrase "six feet under":* Matt So-
niak, "How Did 6 Feet Become the Standard Grave Depth?" *Mental Floss,*
November 29, 2012, http://mentalfloss.com/article/31633/how-did-6
-feet-become-standard-grave-depth.

Page 82, *According to a story in the* Houston Chronicle, *"For those who":* Jennifer
Kimrey, "The Most Interesting Facts about Morticians," *Houston Chronicle,*
http://work.chron.com/interesting-morticians-11175.html.

Page 83, *According to professional gravediggers, shovel slowly and steadily:* Corey
Kilgannon, "The Ones Who Prepare the Ground for the Last Farewell,
New York Times, January 30, 2006, http://www.nytimes.com/2006/01
/30/nyregion/the-ones-who-prepare-the-ground-for-the-last-farewell
.html.

Page 83, *These are adapted from advice given by Britain's Jonny Yaxley:* Xan Rice,
"How to Dig a Perfect Grave: A Day with Britain's Top Undertaker," *New
Republic,* November 16, 2014, https://newrepublic.com/article/120428
/britains-grave-digger-year-how-did-perfect-grave.

Page 84, *In 2016, the second annual Grave Digging Competition:* "Speedy
Shovels Shine in Slovakia," Associated Press, November 10, 2016,
https://www.usnews.com/news/world/articles/2016-11-10/speedy
-shovels-shine-in-slovakias-gravedigging-contest. See also David Moye,
"Grave Diggers Get Down and Dirty at International Competition,"

Huffington Post, November 11, 2016, https://www.huffingtonpost.com
/entry/grave-digging-championship_us_5826164de4b060adb56e370d.

Page 87, *The Environmental Protection Agency (EPA) oversees US laws:* For more
information, see "Burial at Sea," US Environmental Protection Agency,
https://www.epa.gov/ocean-dumping/burial-sea; and the specific EPA
regulation (40 CFR 229.1), https://www.gpo.gov/fdsys/pkg
/CFR-2011-title40-vol25/pdf/CFR-2011-title40-vol25-sec229-1.pdf.

Page 87, *New England Burials at Sea is a Massachusetts company:* For more information on New England Burials at Sea, visit http://www.new
englandburialsatsea.com; my email exchange with Captain Brad White
occurred April 1, 2017.

Page 88, *Osama bin Laden is buried at sea. His body:* Dave Gilson, "What Happens When You're Buried at Sea?" *Mother Jones,* May 9, 2011, http://www
.motherjones.com/environment/2011/05/bin-laden-burial-at-sea.

Chapter 7. Green Burial Containers: Handmade Caskets and Shrouds

Page 89, *"The best caskets are joyful epitaphs in wood":* Steve Maxwell, "Learn
How to Build a Handmade Casket," *Mother Earth News,* April/May 2003,
https://www.motherearthnews.com/diy/how-to-build-a-handmade
-casket-zmaz03amzgoe.

Page 91, *In Ghana, "fantasy coffins" are constructed to represent:* Charlotte Jansen,
"How Ghana's Top Fantasy Coffin Artist Has Put the Fun in Funeral,"
The Guardian, November 24, 2016, https://www.theguardian.com/
world/2016/nov/24/paa-joe-ghana-fantasy-coffin-artist-casket-funeral.

Page 91, *Still, as Mother Nature Network observed, "Producing a new coffin":* Matt
Hickman, "Shelving to Die For," *Mother Nature Network,* June 19, 2009,
https://www.mnn.com/your-home/remodeling-design/blogs/shelving
-to-die-for.

Page 94, *The Green Burial Council declares that a "shroud is suitable":* "What Is
Green Burial?" Green Burial Council, https://greenburialcouncil.org
/home/what-is-green-burial.

Page 98, *If you want to construct your own cardboard coffin:* For a step-by-step
guide to building your own cardboard coffin, download free instructions
at DIYing Free, https://diyingfree.weebly.com/download.html.

Page 99, *The company Coeio produces green burial items that:* For more information on the Infinity Burial Suit and Shroud, visit Coeio, http://coeio.com.

Page 99, *Ecopods are a natural burial chest that was designed by:* For more information on the EcoPod, visit http://www.ecopod.co.uk.

Chapter 8. Green Embalming and Handling the Body

Page 101, *First, embalming is never required by any state:* "Embalming Green," *Elemental Cremation & Burial,* https://www.elementalnw.com/2013/03/14/embalming-green.

Page 102, *Green embalming fluids are made of a variety of nontoxic:* For more on green embalming products, review the following sources: Curtis D. Rostad, "In Search of the Perfect Embalming Chemical, Shepherd's Funeral Supplies, October 20, 2014, http://www.shepherds.ie/news/search-perfect-embalming-chemical; and "Greener Embalming," AGreenerFuneral.org, http://www.agreenerfuneral.org/greener-funerals/embalming/greener-embalming.

Page 104, *Here is a brief summary of the physical stages that occur:* "Rigor Mortis and Other Postmortem Changes," Encyclopedia of Death and Dying, http://www.deathreference.com/Py-Se/Rigor-Mortis-and-Other-Postmortem-Changes.html.

Page 108, *In ancient times, when coins were made out of heavier metals:* Julia Neuberger, *Dying Well: A Guide to Enabling a Good Death* (Boca Raton, FL: CRC Press, 2004), 3.

Page 110, *You can also approach grocery stores and other retail stores:* For help locating retail stores that sell dry ice, visit Airgas, which sells Penguin brand dry ice nationally, http://dryiceideas.com/retail-locator.

Page 110, *Most of all, you must be very careful handling dry ice:* For more advice on how to handle dry ice, see two articles at How Stuff Works: Marshall Brain, "What If I Touched Dry Ice?" March 24, 2008, https://science.howstuffworks.com/touched-dry-ice.htm; and "How Does Dry Ice Work?" April 1, 2000, https://science.howstuffworks.com/innovation/science-questions/question264.htm.

Page 111, *Another option is to use a "cooling blanket":* Lee Webster, *Changing Landscapes: Exploring the Growth of Ethical, Compassionate, and Environmentally Sustainable Green Funeral Service* (Seattle, WA: CreateSpace Independent Publishing Platform, Green Burial Council International, 2017), 58.

Page 112, *For up-to-date information in a state-by-state chart:* Lee Webster and Josh Slocum, *Restoring Families' Right to Choose: The Call for Funeral*

Legislation Change in America (Seattle, WA: CreateSpace Independent Publishing Platform, 2016), a publication of the National Home Funeral Alliance and the Funeral Consumers Alliance. See also, "Quick Guide to Legal Requirements for Home Funerals in Your State," National Home Funeral Alliance, http://homefuneralalliance.org/the-law/quick-guide.

Chapter 9. Conducting a Home Funeral or Green Burial

Page 115, *As Lee Webster, president emeritus of the National Home Funeral Alliance*: Lee Webster, email correspondence with author, January 27, 2018.

Page 128, *For more information and advice on grave maintenance*: "Opening, Closing, and Maintaining of a Green Burial Cemetery," Green Burial Council, 2015, http://greenburialcouncil.org/wp-content/uploads /2015/09/OpeningClosingandMaintenanceFinal.pdf

Chapter 10. Cremation

Page 132, *Dean Fisher, who heads UCLA's Body Donation Program:* Lesley McClurg, "Want to Cut Your Carbon Footprint? Get Liquefied When You're Dead," *KQED,* July 24, 2017, last updated October 16, 2017, https://ww2.kqed.org/futureofyou/2017/09/20/want-to-cut-your -carbon-footprint-get-liquefied-when-youre-dead.

Page 132, *While costs vary, alkaline hydrolysis typically costs:* Ibid.

Page 132, *For instance, the Sierra Club writes, "Lower temperatures help"*: Bob Schildgen, "Hey Mr. Green, Is Alkaline Hydrolysis More Ecofriendly Than Cremation?" *Sierra,* October 27, 2015, http://www.sierraclub.org /sierra/2015-6-november-december/green-life/hey-mr-green-alkaline -hydrolysis-more-ecofriendly.

Page 133, *He writes, "To a great extent the bodies are"*: Lee Webster, *Changing Landscapes: Exploring the Growth of Ethical, Compassionate, and Environmentally Sustainable Green Funeral Service* (Seattle, WA: CreateSpace Independent Publishing Platform, Green Burial Council International, 2017), 177.

Page 133, *As of early 2018, twelve US states consider alkaline*: "Legislative: State Legislation," Bio Cremation, http://biocremationinfo.com/legislative.

Page 136, *The Georgia-based company Eternal Reefs takes human ashes:* "Eco-Afterlife: Green Burial Options," *Scientific American,* https://www

.scientificamerican.com/article/eco-afterlife-green-buria. See also the
Eternal Reefs company website, http://www.eternalreefs.com.

Page 136, *Several companies now offer something called a bio urn:* For more information, visit the websites of the following companies: BioUrn,
http://www.biourn4pets.com/biourn-for-people; Bios Urn, https://urn
abios.com; and the Living Urn, https://www.thelivingurn.com.

Page 136, *the company Let Your Love Grow has solved this problem by mixing:* Let
Your Love Grow, http://www.letyourlovegrow.com.

Page 136, *Artist Nadine Jarvis's designs have turned cremation ashes:* Amanda
Green, "Ten Things Your Ashes Can Do after You Die," *Mental Floss,* July
26, 2013, http://mentalfloss.com/article/51905/10-amazing-things
-your-ashes-can-do-after-you-die.

Page 137, *For instance, I know a woman who, after her fiftieth birthday:* This
story is adapted from a previously published article: Elizabeth Fournier,
"Recycling Comes from Within," Naturally Savvy, November 10, 2011,
http://naturallysavvy.com/live/recycling-comes-from-within.

Chapter 11: A Green Goodbye: Memorials and Mementos

Page 142, *Another reason to avoid cut flowers is that they have a high:* Jennifer
Grayson, "Eco Etiquette: What's the Environmental Cost of Cut
Flowers?" *Huffington Post,* February 9, 2012, last updated April 9, 2012,
https://www.huffingtonpost.com/jennifer-grayson/eco-etiquette-whats
-the-e_b_1264647.html.

Page 142, *Seed cards are made from completely biodegradable natural fibers:* A
number of companies produce seed cards. Some include Passages International, http://www.passagesinternational.com/keepsakes-remembrances;
Botanical Paperworks, https://www.botanicalpaperworks.com; Bloomin,
https://bloomin.com; and Symphony Handmade Papers, http://seed
cards.com.

Page 144, *For a sustainable option, use biodegradable, helium "dove" balloons:*
Two companies that sell biodegradable dove balloons are Bio Doves,
http://www.biodoves.com, and Just Artifacts, https://www.justartifacts
.net/doveballoons.html. You can also find them for sale online.

RESOURCES

Information

Aging with Dignity (www.agingwithdignity.org): Changing the way we talk about and plan for end-of-life care inspired by Mother Teresa of Calcutta.

Caring Info (www.caringinfo.org): Free resource on end-of-life care run by the National Hospice and Palliative Care Organization.

Conscious Elders Network (www.consciouselders.org): A nonprofit organization dedicated to educating through the environmental stewardship of our society's living elders.

Cornerstone Funeral Services (www.cornerstonefuneral .com): The first green funeral home in Oregon hosts a website with plentiful information.

Crossings: Caring for Our Own at Death (www.crossings.net): A home funeral and green burial online resource center.

Death Cafe (http://deathcafe.com): Promotes and facilitates gatherings in cities across the country to discuss death with no agenda or objectives except sharing and learning.

Dying Matters (www.dyingmatters.org): A website raising the awareness of death, dying, and bereavement.

Encyclopedia of Death and Dying (www.deathreference.com): What it says, an encyclopedia of death and dying.

Final Passages (http://finalpassages.org): An online resource for death midwifery and home funeral guidance.

Funeral Consumers Alliance (https://funerals.org): A thorough guide providing funeral consumers with fully monitored funeral-industry information.

Green Burial Council (http://greenburialcouncil.org): A nonprofit organization working to encourage environmentally sustainable death care.

Green Burial Naturally (www.greenburialnaturally.org/blog): Reflections on green burial by Ann Hoffner, author of *The Natural Burial Cemetery Guide*.

Hospice Foundation of America (http://hospicefoundation .org): This website provides information on issues related to hospice and end-of-life care.

National End-of-Life Doula Alliance (www.nedalliance.org): A standard-setting membership organization that promotes end-of-life doulas as caregivers, volunteers, and professionals.

National Funeral Directors Association (NFDA; www.nfda .org): A source of expertise and professional resources for all facets of funeral service.

National Home Funeral Alliance (NHFA; http://homefuneral
alliance.org): A nonprofit organization sharing information and directories for everything related to home
funerals.

Natural End Map (www.naturalend.com): An online di-
rectory map to natural funeral service providers,
end-of-life assistants, home funeral guides, and green
cemeteries.

Natural Transitions (www.naturaltransitions.org): A nonprofit resource center providing education on conscious, holistic, and green approaches to end of life.

Seven Ponds (www.sevenponds.com): A contemporary
website for those who wish to celebrate memory and
personalize the end of death.

GREEN BURIAL GROUNDS IN THE UNITED STATES AND CANADA

*F*or the definitions of these types of burial grounds (in parenthesis), see chapter 6, "The Three Categories of Green Burial Grounds" (page 74). At the end of this list of US states, I include green burial grounds in two Canadian provinces: British Columbia and Ontario.

This list of green burial grounds is based on "Green Burial Cemeteries in the US & Canada," created by Lee Webster and published by the nonprofit New Hampshire Funeral Resources, Education & Advocacy (NHFREA, http://www.nhfuneral.org/publications.html), which is continually updated; visit the website for the up-to-date version.

ALABAMA

Forest Lawn Memorial Gardens (Hybrid)
10000 Celeste Road
Saraland, AL 36571
www.ascensionfuneralgroup.com
(251) 675-0824

Garden of Oaks at Spring Hill (Hybrid)
600 Pierce Road
Mobile, AL 36695
www.ascensionfuneralgroup.com
(251) 639-0962

The Good Earth Burial Ground
(Natural preserve in progress)
101 Hazel Wood Drive
Hazel Green, AL 35750
www.thegoodearthllc.com
(256) 655-2170

Sunset Memorial Park (Hybrid)
1700 Barrington Road
Midland City, AL 36350
www.sunsetmemorialpark.com
(334) 983-6604

Tallapoosa County Memorial Gardens (Hybrid)
21927 Highway 280
Dadeville, AL 36853
http://alabamafuneralhomes.com
(256) 825-0038

ARIZONA

Marana Mortuary Cemetery
(Hybrid)
12146 W Barnett Road
Marana, AZ 85653
http://maranamortuarycemetery.com
(520) 682-9900

Sunwest Cemetery (Hybrid)
12525 NW Grand Avenue
El Mirage, AZ 85335
www.heritagefuneralchapels.com
(623) 974-2054

ARKANSAS

Gracelawn Memorial Park
(Hybrid)
3000 Oak Lane
Van Buren, AR 72956
(479) 462-7555

CALIFORNIA

Cayetano Natural Burial Ground at Tolocay (Hybrid)
411 Coombsville Road
Napa, CA 94559
www.tulocaycemetery.org
(707) 252-4727

Davis Cemetery and Arboretum (Hybrid)
820 Pole Line Road
Davis, CA 95618
http://daviscemetery.org
(530) 756-7807

Eternal Meadow at Woodlawn Cemetery (Hybrid)
1847 14th Street
Santa Monica, CA 90404
www.smgov.net/departments/cemetery
(310) 458-8717

Forever Fernwood (Natural)
301 Tennessee Valley Road
Mill Valley, CA 94941
www.foreverfernwood.com
(415) 383-7100

Greenlawn Memorial Park
(Hybrid)
1100 El Camino Real
Colma, CA 94014
www.greenlawnmemorialpark.com
(650) 755-7622

Hillside Memorial Park
(Hybrid)
6001 W Centinela Avenue
Los Angeles, CA 90045
www.hillsidememorial.org
(310) 641-0707

Joshua Tree Memorial Park
(Hybrid)
60121 29 Palms Highway
Joshua Tree, CA 92252
www.joshuatreememorialpark.com
(760) 366-9210

The Meadow/Westwood Hills Memorial Park (Hybrid)
2720 Cold Springs Road
Placerville, CA 95667
www.facebook.com/pages/Westwood
-Hills-Memorial-Park-Inc/11611
4788417264
(530) 622-2223

Pleasant Hills Cemetery
(Hybrid)
1700 Pleasant Hill Road
Sebastopol, CA 95472
http://pleasanthillsmemorialpark.com
(707) 869-2842

Purissima Cemetery (Natural)
1103 Verde Road
Half Moon Bay, CA 94019
steelmantowncemetery.com
/purissima.html
(609) 628-2297

Sunset Lawn Chapel of the Chimes Cemetery (Hybrid)
4701 Marysville Boulevard
Sacramento, CA 95838
http://sunsetlawn.chapelofthechimes
.com
(916) 922-5833

COLORADO

Crestone Cemetery (Natural Burial Project)
108 West Galena Avenue
Crestone, CO 81131
http://informedfinalchoices.org
/crestone/about-ceolp/
(719) 256-4313

Evergreen Memorial Park
(Hybrid)
26624 N. Turkey Creek Road
Evergreen, CO 80439
www.evergreenmemorialpark.com
(303) 674-7750

Roselawn Cemetery (Natural)
2718 East Mulberry Street
Fort Collins, CO 80524
www.fcgov.com/cemeteries
(970) 221-6810

Seven Stones Botanical Garden (Natural)
9635 N Rampart Range Road
Littleton, CO 80125
www.discoversevenstones.com
(307) 717-7117

CONNECTICUT

Wooster Cemetery (Hybrid)
20 Ellsworth Avenue
Danbury, CT 06810
www.wooster-cemetery.com
(203) 748-8529

DISTRICT OF COLUMBIA

Historic Congressional Cemetery (Hybrid)
1801 East Street SE
Washington, DC 20003
www.congressionalcemetery.org
(202) 543-0539

FLORIDA

Brooksville Cemetery (Hybrid)
1275 Olmes Road
Brooksville, FL 34601
www.ci.brooksville.fl.us/index.php
?option=com_content&view=article
&id=69&Itemid=4
(352) 540-3806

Eternal Rest Memories Park
(Hybrid)
2966 Belcher Road
Dunedin, FL 34698
www.facebook.com/pages/Eternal
-Rest-Memorial-Park/171925
279594658
(727) 733-2300

Glendale Memorial Nature Preserve (Natural)
297 Railroad Avenue
DeFuniak Springs, FL 32433
http://glendalenaturepreserve.org
(850) 859-2141

Green Meadows at Brooksville Cemetery (Hybrid)
1275 Olmes Road
Brooksville, FL 34601
(352) 544-5455

Heartwood Preserve
(Conservation)
4100 Starkey Boulevard
Trinity, FL 34655
www.heartwoodpreserve.com
(727) 376-5111

Prairie Creek Conservation Cemetery (Conservation)
7204 SE County Road 234
Gainesville, FL 32641
http://conservationburialinc.org
(352) 317-7307

Riverview Memorial Gardens
(Hybrid)
371 Highway 1 North
Cocoa, FL 32926
www.riverviewmemorialcemetery.com
(321) 632-9050

GEORGIA

Honey Creek Woodlands
(Natural)
2625 Highway 212 SW
Conyers, GA 30094
www.honeycreekwoodlands.com
(770) 483-7535

Milton Fields (Natural)
1150 Birmingham Road
Milton, GA 30004
https://miltonfieldsgeorgia.com
(770) 751-1445

HAWAII

Valley Isle Memorial Park Cemetery (Hybrid)
105 Waiale Road
Wailuku, Maui, HI 96793
www.ballardfamilymortuaries.com
(808) 244-4911

IDAHO

Mountain View Green Cemetery (Natural)
3770 Lemhi Road
Leadore, ID 83464
www.mountainviewgreencemetery
.com
(208) 768-7404

ILLINOIS

Pleasant Grove Memorial Park (Hybrid)
31 Memorial Drive
Murphysboro, IL 62966
www.crainsonline.com/services
/green-funerals
(618) 687-1145

Roselawn Memorial Park (Hybrid)
924 South 6th Street
Springfield, IL 62703
www.roselawninfo.com
(217) 525-1661

Sunset Memorial Park and Nature's Way (Hybrid)
3901 N Vermillion Street
Danville, IL 61834
www.sunsetfuneralhome.com
(217) 442-2874

Windridge Memorial Park and Nature Sanctuary (Hybrid)
7014 S Rawson Bridge Road
Cary, IL 60013
www.burialplanning.com/cemeteries
/windridge-memorial-park
(847) 639-3883

INDIANA

Kessler Woods at Washington Park North Cemetery (Hybrid)
2706 Kessler Boulevard W Drive
Indianapolis, IN 46228
https://flannerbuchanan.com
/locations/kessler-woods
(317) 259-1253

Oak Hill Cemetery (Natural)
392 W Oak Hill Road
Crawfordsville, IN 47933
www.oakhillcemeteryof
crawfordsville.com
(765) 362-6602

Porter Rea Cemetery (Hybrid)
65065 Pine Road
North Liberty, IN, 46614
(574) 656-4587

The Preserve at Springvale Cemetery (Hybrid)
2580 Schuyler Avenue
Lafayette, IN 47905
www.facebook.com/Spring-Vale
-Cemetery-119472408066143
(765) 742-7028

White Oak Cemetery (Hybrid)
1200 W 7th Street
Bloomington, IN 47404
https://bloomington.in.gov/locations
/white-oak-cemetery
(812) 349-3498

KANSAS

Bel Aire Ascension Cemetery
(Hybrid)
424 N Broadway
Wichita, KS 67202
http://catholicdioceseofwichita.org
/catholic-cemeteries/locations
(316) 722-1971

Heart Land Prairie Cemetery
(Natural)
2474 Arrowhead Road
New Cambria, KS 67470
www.heartlandprairiecemetery.org
(785) 829-7609

Highland Cemetery (Hybrid)
5000 W 65th Street
Prairie Village, KS 66208
www.highlandcemeteryprairie
village.com
(913) 722-0100

**Lincoln City Cemetery
Catholic** (Hybrid)
111 E Elm Street
Lincoln Center, KS 67455
(785) 524-4549

Mount Muncie Cemetery
(Hybrid)
1500 N 8th Street
Lansing, KS 66043
www.kansastravel.org/mountmuncie
cemetery.htm
(913) 727-1935

Oak Hill Cemetery (Hybrid)
1605 Oak Hill Avenue
Lawrence, KS 66044
https://lawrenceks.org/lprd/parks
/oakhillcemetery
(785) 832-3451

MAINE

Burr Cemetery (Hybrid)
56 Durham Road
Freeport, ME 04032
www.cremationmaine.com/Burr
Cemetery.html
(207) 865-3940

Cedar Brook Burial Ground
(Natural)
175 Boothby Road
Limington, ME 04049
http://mainegreencemetery.com
(207) 637-2085

**Rainbow's End Natural
Burial Ground** (Natural)
48 Mill Creek Road
Orrington, ME 04474
www.orrington.govoffice.com
/index.asp?SEC=EE1C648A
-457E-4245-9A5D-84BA8963CD0
3&Type=B_BASIC
(207) 825-3843

MARYLAND

Bestgate Memorial Park
(Hybrid)
814 Bestgate Road
Annapolis, MD 21401
www.lastingtributesfuneralcare.com
/what-we-do/going-green
(410) 841-6255

MASSACHUSETTS

Mount Auburn Cemetery
(Hybrid)
580 Mount Auburn Street
Cambridge, MA 02138
http://mountauburn.org
(617) 547-7105

MICHIGAN

Eagle Harbor Cemetery
(Hybrid)
321 Centre Street
Eagle Harbor, MI 49950
www.eagleharbortwp.org
/departments/cemetery
(960) 289-4407

Forest Lawn Cemetery (Hybrid)
11851 Van Dyke Street
Detroit, MI 48234
(313) 921-6960

Hebrew Memorial Chapel
(Natural)
26640 Greenfield Road
Oak Park, MI 48237
www.hebrewmemorial.org
(248) 543-1622

Marble Park Cemetery (Hybrid)
520 W Main Street
Milan, MI 48160
http://marbleparkcemetery.com
(734) 439-5660

Mount Carmel Cemetery
(Hybrid)
135 Superior Boulevard
Wyandotte, MI 48192
www.cfcsdetroit.org/cemetery
(734) 285-1722

Peninsula Township Cemetery
(Hybrid)
13235 Center Road
Traverse City, MI 49686
www.peninsulatownship.com
/cemeteries.html
(231) 223-7321

The Preserve at All Saints
Cemetery (Hybrid)
4401 Nelsey Road
Waterford, MI 48329-1057
www.michigannaturalburial.com
(248) 623-9633

Ridgeview Memorial Gardens
(Hybrid)
5151 8th Avenue SW
Grandville, MI 49418
www.ridgeviewmemorialgardens.com
(616) 249-8439

MINNESOTA

Mound Cemetery of Brooklyn
Center (Hybrid)
3515 69th Avenue
North Brooklyn Center, MN 55429
www.moundcemetery.com
(952) 935-0954

Prairie Oaks Memorial Eco Gardens (Natural)
8225 Argenta Trail
Inver Grove Heights, MN 55077
www.prairieoaksmemorialeco
gardens.org
(651) 300-5934

MISSOURI

Bellefontaine Cemetery
(Hybrid)
4947 W Florissant Avenue
St. Louis, MO 63115
http://bellefontainecemetery.org
/cemetery-services/green-burial
-options
(314) 381-0750

Gates to Heaven Cemeteries
(Natural)
255 Jackett Road
Seligman, MO 65745
www.facebook.com/gatestoheaven
cemetery
(417) 341-1800

Green Acres Cemetery (Natural)
1400 S Hickory School Road
Rocheport, MO 65279
www.mo-greenburial.com
(888) 325-2653

NEVADA

Eastside Memorial Park
(Natural)
1600 Buckeye Road
Minden, NV 89423
www.eastsidememorialpark.com
(775) 782-2215

The Gardens (Hybrid)
2949 Austin Highway
Fallon, NV 89406
www.thegardensfuneralhome.com
(775) 423-8928

NEW HAMPSHIRE

Chocorua Cemetery (Hybrid)
12 Deer Hill Road
Tamworth, NH 03886
(603) 323-8617

Laurel Hill Cemetery (Hybrid)
61 Island Street
Wilton, NH 03086
(603) 654-6602

Monadnock Quaker Meeting Friends Natural Burial Ground (Natural)
3 Davidson Road
Jaffrey, NH 03452
(603) 532-6203

Richmond Cemetery (Hybrid)
70 Athol Road
Richmond, NH 03470
www.richmond.nh.gov/index.asp?SE
C=D7084C30-6374-4D35-A9B0-18
2EAAADF0ED&Type=B_BASIC
(603) 903-2184

Tamworth Town Cemetery
(Hybrid)
Hollow Hill Road
Tamworth, NH 03886
(603) 323-8617

NEW JERSEY

Maryrest Catholic Cemetery
(Hybrid)
770 Darlington Avenue
Mahwah, NJ 07430
www.rcancem.org/maryrest
-cemetery-a-mausoleum
(201) 327-7011

Steelmantown Cemetery
(Natural)
101 Steelmantown Road
Woodbine, NJ 08270
www.steelmantowncemetery.com
(609) 628-2297

**Union Cemetery at Mays
Landing** (Natural)
195 Route 50
Mays Landing, NJ 08330
www.theunioncemetery.com
(609) 625-7571

NEW MEXICO

**New Mexico La Puerta Natural
Burial Ground** (Natural)
601 Griegos Road NW
Albuquerque, NM 87107
www.naturalburialnewmexico.com
(505) 716-2543

NEW YORK

**Ascension Garden St. Francis
Meadow** (Natural)
1900 Pinnacle Road
Henrietta, NY 14467
www.holysepulchre.org/about/news
/2013-11-27/holy-sepulchre
-cemetery-ascension-garden-1st
-catholic-cemeteries-new-york
(585) 697-1122

**Fultonville Natural Burial
Ground** (Natural)
Upper Mohawk Street
Fultonville, NY 12072
www.facebook.com/fultonville
cemetery
(518) 265-7577

**Greensprings Natural
Cemetery**
293 Irish Hill Road
Newfield, NY 14867
www.naturalburial.org
(607) 564-7577

Holy Sepulchre Cemetery
(Natural)
2461 Lake Avenue
Rochester, NY 14612
www.holysepulchre.org
(585) 458-4110

**Most Holy Redeemer
Cemetery / Katari Meadow
Natural Burial Preserve**
(Hybrid)
2501 Troy Schenectady Road
Schenectady, NY 12309
www.capitaldistrictcemetaries.org
(518) 374-5319

Mount Hope Cemetery
(Hybrid)
1133 Mount Hope Avenue
Rochester, NY 14620
www.cityofrochester.gov/mounthope
(585) 428-7999

Oakwood Cemetery (Hybrid)
50 101st Street
Troy, NY 12180
www.oakwoodcemetery.org
(518) 272-7520

Rhinebeck Cemetery (Natural)
3 Mill Road
Rhinebeck, NY 12572
http://friendsofrhinebeckcemetery.org
(845) 876-3961

Rosendale Cemetery (Hybrid)
793 Springtown Road
Tillson, NY 12486
www.rosendalecemetery.com/natural
-burial.html
(845) 658-9042

Sleepy Hollow Cemetery
(Hybrid)
540 N Broadway
Sleepy Hollow, NY 10591
http://sleepyhollowcemetery.org
(914) 631-0081

St. Peter's Cemetery (Hybrid)
241 Broadway
Saratoga Springs, NY 12866
www.stpetersaratoga.com/st-peters
-cemetery.html
(518) 584-2375

Vale Cemetery (Natural)
907 State Street
Schenectady, NY 12307
www.valecemetery.org
(518) 346-0423

White Haven Memorial Park
(Natural)
210 Marsh Road
Pittsford, NY 14534
www.whitehavenmemorialpark.com
(585) 586-5250

NORTH CAROLINA

Carolina Memorial Sanctuary
(Conservation)
195 Blessed Way
Mills River, NC 28759
www.carolinamemorialsanctuary.org
(828) 782-7283

Forest Lawn Memorial Park
(Hybrid)
538 Tracy Grove Road
Hendersonville, NC 28792
www.forestlawnnc.com
(828) 692-9188

Green Hills Cemetery (Hybrid)
24 New Leicester Highway
Asheville, NC 28806
www.greenhillscemeteryasheville.com
(828) 252-9831

**Mordecai's Meadow at
Oakwood Cemetery** (Hybrid)
701 Oakwood Avenue
Raleigh, NC 27601
http://historicoakwoodcemetery.org
/green-burials.asp
(919) 832-6077

Pine Forest Memorial Gardens (Natural)
770 Stadium Drive
Wake Forest, NC 27587
https://pineforestmemorial.com
(919) 556-6776

OHIO

Calvary Cemetery Dayton St. Kateri Preserve (Natural)
1625 Calvary Drive
Dayton, OH 45409
www.calvarycemeterydayton.org
(937) 293-1221

Canton Cemetery Association North Lawn Cemetery (Natural)
4927 Cleveland Avenue NW
Canton, OH 44709
www.cantoncemeteryassociation.net
(330) 494-0641

Foxfield Preserve Nature Cemetery (Conservation)
9877 Alabama Avenue SW
Wilmot, OH 44689
(330) 763-1331

Glen Forest Natural Burial Cemetery (Natural)
US Route 68 N
Yellow Springs, OH 45387
(937) 767-2460

Kokosing Nature Preserve
(Conservation)
306 Gaskin Avenue
Gambier, OH 43022
www.kenyon.edu/directories
/offices-services/philander-chase
-conservancy/kokosing-nature
-preserve
(740) 427-5040

Preble Memory Gardens Cemetery (Conservation)
3377 US Route 35 E
West Alexandria, OH 45381
www.greenburialatpmg.com
(937) 839-4476

Spring Grove Cemetery
(Hybrid)
4521 Grove Avenue
Cincinnati, OH 45232
www.springgrove.org
(513) 681-7526

OKLAHOMA

Green Haven Cemetery
(Natural)
2400 S Coyle Road
Stillwater OK 74076
www.greenhavencemetery.org
(405) 747-9642

Green Tree Burial Grounds
(Natural)
218 South Ranchette Road
Mead, OK 73449
www.greentreeburialgrounds.org
(405) 550-265

Woodland Memorial Park
(Hybrid)
1200 N Cleveland
Sand Springs, OK 74063
www.dillonsmithfuneralservice.com
(918) 245-4142

OREGON

Eugene Masonic Cemetery
(Hybrid)
2575 University Street
Eugene, OR 97403
www.eugenemasoniccemetery.com
(541) 684-0949

Gibson Cemetery (Hybrid)
SE Wildcat Mountain Road and
Crane Road
Estacada, OR 97023
(503) 730-0142

IOOF Eastwood Cemetery
(Hybrid)
1581 Siskiyou Boulevard
Medford, OR 97504
(541) 774-2400

Mountain View Cemetery
(Hybrid)
440 Normal Avenue
Ashland, OR 97520
www.ashland.or.us/Page.asp?Nav
ID=13663
(541) 482-3826

**Mount Calvary Catholic
Cemetery** (Hybrid)
333 SW Skyline Boulevard
Portland, OR 97221
www.ccpdxor.com/st-francis-green
-burial
(503) 292-6621

Oak Hill Cemetery (Hybrid)
88558 Oak Hill Cemetery Road
Eugene, OR 97402
www.oakhillonline.com
(541) 689-7800

Rest Lawn Memorial Park
(Hybrid)
94335 Territorial Highway Park
Junction City, OR 97448
www.restlawnonline.com/natural
-burial
(541) 998-5810

Riverview Cemetery (Hybrid)
8421 SW Macadam Avenue
Portland, OR 97219
www.riverviewcemeteryfuneralhome
.com
(503) 246-6488

Rose City Cemetery (Hybrid)
5625 NE Fremont Street
Portland, OR 97213
www.rosecityfuneralhome.com
(503) 281-3821

**Valley Memorial Park &
Funeral Home** (Hybrid)
3809 SE Tualatin Valley Highway
Hillsboro, OR 97123
www.valleymemorialoregon.com
(503) 648-5444

PENNSYLVANIA

Beechwood Cemetery (Hybrid)
Bensalem Boulevard at Hulmeville
Road
Bensalem, PA 19020
www.beechwoodcemetery
bensalem.com
(215) 639-8970

Doylestown Cemetery (Hybrid)
215 East Court Street
Doylestown, PA 18901
www.doylestowncemetery.com
(215) 348-3911

Gethsemane Cemetery (Hybrid)
3139 Kutztown Road
Laureldale, PA 19605
www.gethcem.com
(610) 929-2613

Green Meadow at Fountain Hill (Natural)
1121 Graham Street
Fountain Hill, PA 18015
www.greenmeadowpa.org
(610) 868-4840

Holy Savior Cemetery (Hybrid)
4629 Bakerstown Road
Gibsonia, PA 15044
http://www.ccapgh.org/holy-savior.asp
(724) 625-3822

Oakwood Cemetery (Hybrid)
600 N Oakland Avenue
Sharon, PA 16146
www.oakwoodcemeterypa.org
/grave-spaces
(724) 346-4775

Paxtang Cemetery (Hybrid)
401 Kelso Street
Harrisburg, PA 17111
www.paxtangcemetery.com
(717) 564-2110

Penn Forest Natural Burial Park (Natural)
118 Colorado Street
Verona, PA 15147
www.pennforestcemetery.com
(412) 265-4606

West Laurel Hill Cemetery (Hybrid)
215 Belmont Avenue
Bala Cynwyd, PA 19004
http://westlaurelhill.com
(610) 664-1591

West View Cemetery (Hybrid)
4920 Perry Highway
Pittsburgh, PA 15229
https://rodefshalom.org/about
/westview-cemetery
(412) 931-1600

RHODE ISLAND

Arnold Mills Cemetery (Hybrid)
680 Nate Whipple Highway
Cumberland, RI 02864
www.arnoldmillscemetery.com
(401) 333-5437

SOUTH CAROLINA

Dust to Dust Green Burial Cemetery (Natural)
205 Nulty Crossing
Swansea, SC 29160
www.dusttodustcemetery.com
(803) 568-5552

Greenhaven Preserve (Natural)
1701 Vanboklen Road
Eastover, SC 29044
http://greenhavenpreserve.com
(803) 403-9561

Ramsey Creek Preserve
(Conservation)
390 Cobb Bridge Road
Westminster, SC 29693
www.memorialecosystems.com
(864) 647-7798

Saluda Rest Preserve (Natural)
113 Edwards Road
Marietta, SC 29661
www.facebook.com/SaludaRest
(864) 884-9503

SOUTH DAKOTA

**Mt. Pleasant Cemetery
Association** (Hybrid)
2001 E 12th Street
Sioux Falls, SD 57103
www.mtpleasantsf.com
(605) 339-4760

TENNESSEE

Elmwood Cemetery (Hybrid)
824 S Dudley Street
Memphis, TN 38104
www.elmwoodcemetery.org
(901) 774-3212

**Larkspur Conservation
Preserve** (Conservation)
Bear Carr Road
Westmoreland, TN 37212
www.larkspurconservation.org
(615) 854-0010

Maury Memorial Gardens
(Hybrid)
611 Bear Creek Pike
Columbia, TN 38401

www.maurymemorial.com/m
/ingroundburial.html
(931) 840-4875

**Narrow Ridge Natural Burial
Preserve** (Natural)
1936 Liberty Hill Road
Washburn, TN 37888
https://narrowridge.org/about
/natural-burial-preserve
(865) 497-2753

TEXAS

Countryside Memorial Park
(Hybrid)
331 Cemetery Lane
La Vernia, TX 78121
http://countrysidememorialpark.com
(210) 828-1233

**Eloise Woods Community
Natural Burial Park** (Natural)
115 Northside Lane
Cedar Creek, TX 78612
www.eloisewoods.com
(512) 796-5240

Ethician Family Cemetery
(Natural)
1401 19th Street
Huntsville, TX 77340
http://ethicianfamilycemetery.org
(936) 581-4302

North Belton Cemetery
(Hybrid)
1500 N Main Street
Belton, TX 76513
(254) 939-8123

Our Lady of the Rosary Cemetery & Prayer Gardens
(Hybrid)
330 Berry Lane
Georgetown, TX 78626
www.olotr.com
(512) 863-8411

Tranquility Oaks Cemetery
(Hybrid)
22302 Hildebrandt Rd
Spring, TX 77389
www.addisonfuneralhomes.com
(281) 350-0998

UTAH

Aultorest Memorial Park
(Hybrid)
836 36th Street
Ogden, UT 84403
www.leavittsmortuary.com
(801) 394-5556

Memorial Lakeview Cemetery
(Hybrid)
1640 E Lakeview Drive
Bountiful, UT 84010
www.memorialutah.com/locations
/lakeview
(801) 298-1564

VERMONT

Meetinghouse Hill Cemetery
(Hybrid)
430 Orchard Street
Brattleboro, VT 05301
www.countyoffice.org
/meetinghouse-hill-cemetery
-west-brattleboro-vt-da0
(802) 257-0712

VIRGINIA

Coolsprings Cemetery at Holy Cross Abbey Monastery
(Natural)
901 Cool Spring Lane
Berryville, VA 22611
www.virginiatrappists.org
(540) 955-4816

Duck Run Natural Cemetery
(Natural)
3173 Spotswood Trail
Harrisonburg, VA 22801
http://duckruncemetery.com
(540) 432-8650

Forest Rest Natural Cemetery
(Natural)
5970 Grassy Hill Road
Boones Mill, VA 24065
http://forestrestnaturalcemetery.com
(540) 334-5410

The Meadow Natural Burial Ground (Natural)
959 Ross Road
Lexington, VA 24450
http://themeadowlexingtonva.com
(540) 460-4180

WASHINGTON

Cedar Lawns Memorial Park
(Hybrid)
7200 180th Avenue NE
Redmond, WA 98052
www.dignitymemorial.com/cedar
-lawns-funeral-home/en-us/index.page
(425) 885-2414

Fern Prairie Cemetery (Hybrid)
25700 NE Robinson Road
Camas, WA 98607
www.fpcemetery.org
(360) 833-9176

Herland Forest (Natural)
55 Windward Lane
Wahkiacus, WA 98670
www.herlandforest.org
(509) 369-2000

**The Meadow Natural Burial
Grounds** (Natural)
5700 Northwest Drive
Ferndale, WA 98248
http://molesfarewelltributes.com/77
/The_Meadow_at_Greenacres.html
(360) 384-3401

**White Eagle Memorial
Preserve Cemetery**
(Conservation)
401 Ekone Road
Goldendale, WA 98620
http://naturalburialground.org
(206) 383-3285

Woodlawn Cemetery (Hybrid)
7509 Riverview Road
Snohomish, WA 98290
http://woodlawncemetery
snohomish.com/Woodlawn
_Cemetery/Green_Burial_At
_Woodlawn.html
(360) 568-5560

WISCONSIN

Circle Cemetery (Natural)
5354 Meadowvale Road
Barneveld, WI 53507
www.circlesanctuary.org
(608) 924-2216

Forest Home Cemetery
 (Hybrid)
2405 W Forest Home Avenue
Milwaukee, WI 53215
www.foresthomecemetery.com
(414) 645-2632

Greenwood Cemetery (Hybrid)
2615 W Cleveland Avenue
Milwaukee, WI 53215
www.greenwoodjewishcemetery.org
(414) 645-1390

Natural Path Sanctuary
(Natural)
The Farley Center
2299 Spring Rose Road
Verona, WI 53593
http://naturalpathsanctuary.org
(608) 845-8724

**Prairie Green Section of
Greenwood Jewish Cemetery**
(Natural)
2615 W Cleveland Avenue
Milwaukee, WI 53215
www.greenwoodjewishcemetery.org
/jewish-green-burial-milwaukee
-wisconsin
(414) 645-1390

Prairie Home Cemetery
(Hybrid)
605 S Prairie Avenue
Waukesha, WI 53186
www.prairiehomecemetery.com
(262) 524-3540

CANADIAN PROVINCES

BRITISH COLUMBIA

Denman Island Natural Burial Cemetery (Natural)
6400 Denman Road
Denman Island, BC V0R 1T0
http://dinbc.ca
(250) 335-1786

Mountain View Cemetery
(Hybrid)
5455 Fraser Street
Vancouver, BC V5W 2Z3
mountain.view@vancouver.ca
(604) 325-2646

Royal Oak Burial Park (Hybrid)
4673 Falaise Drive
Victoria, BC V8Y 1B4
www.robp.ca
(250) 658-5621

ONTARIO

Cobourg Union Cemetery
(Hybrid)
Elgin Street W
Cobourg, ON K9A 4L3
www.ecoburials.ca
(905) 372-8687

Duffin Meadows Cemetery
(Hybrid)
2505 Brock Road
Pickering, ON L1V 2P8
www.mountpleasantgroup.com
(905) 427-3385

Fairview Cemetery (Hybrid)
4501 Stanley Avenue
Niagara Falls, ON L2E 4Z6
https://niagarafalls.ca/city-hall
/municipal-works/cemetery
/locations-and-histories/fairview.aspx
(950) 354-4721

Meadowvale Cemetery (Hybrid)
7732 Mavis Road
Brampton, ON L6Y 5L5
www.mountpleasantgroup.com
(905) 451-3716

INDEX

Page references given in *italics* indicate illustrations or material contained in their captions.

ABOUT THE AUTHOR

*E*lizabeth Fournier owns and operates Cornerstone Funeral Services in Boring, Oregon, where she is affectionately known as the Green Reaper for her green burial advocacy. She serves on the Advisory Board for the Green Burial Council, the environmental certification organization setting the standard for green burial in North America. She is also the author of *The Green Reaper: Memoirs of an Eco-Mortician*. She lives on a farm with her husband, daughter, and many rescue goats and sheep.

You can connect with Elizabeth here:
www.elizabethfournier.com and
www.cornerstonefuneral.com
Facebook: greenburialportland
Twitter: @elizfournier
Instagram: elizabethgreenreaper